2, A

Arth

Geo 3

$\sqrt{2 \times A + b}$

$12\sqrt{5.781020089 \times 10^{24}}$

$= 115.744502\ 1$

RENEWALS 458-4574

DATE DUE

APR 15			
DEC 8			
MAY 10			
GAYLORD			PRINTED IN U.S.A

Measuring and Managing Derivative Market Risk

Measuring and Managing Derivative Market Risk

David Lawrence

INTERNATIONAL THOMSON BUSINESS PRESS

I(T)P An International Thomson Publishing Company

London • Bonn • Boston • Johannesburg • Madrid • Melbourne • Mexico City • New York • Paris
Singapore • Tokyo • Toronto • Albany, NY • Belmont, CA • Cincinnati, OH • Detroit, MI

Measuring and Managing Derivative Market Risk

Copyright © 1996 David Lawrence

First published 1996 by International Thomson Business Press

I ⓣ P A division of International Thomson Publishing Inc.
The ITP logo is a trademark under licence

British Library Cataloguing-in-Publication Data
A catalogue record for this book is available from the British Library

First edition 1996

Typeset by Hodgson Williams Associates, Tunbridge Wells and Cambridge
Printed in the UK by T.J. Press (Padstow) Ltd., Padstow, Cornwall

ISBN 1-86152-006-9

International Thomson Business Press
Berkshire House
168-173 High Holdborn
London WC1V 7aa
UK

International Thomson Business Press
20 Park Plaza
14th Floor
Boston MA 02116
USA

Contents

CHAPTER ONE

Introduction

1.1 General Outline

The management of price risk has become a matter of growing concern, not only within the financial community itself, but also amongst the regulators and legislators. In the mid-1990s, a great deal of publicity was given to a number of cases where corporations lost substantial sums on derivative transactions. Fortunately, such losses are not an unavoidable consequence of entering into a derivative transaction, but rather stem from a lack of knowledge of the exact price risk involved. These cases highlight the need for a greater dissemination of knowledge on derivative instruments throughout the financial community.

The need for an exact analysis of price risk is a relatively recent phenomenon. There were many approximate measures which sufficed in the past. However, there has been a tremendous growth in the volume of derivatives during the 1990s, so that it is estimated that the total of all the notional amounts now runs into tens of trillions of dollars. Needless to say, an inaccurately estimated risk, even expressed as a small percentage of these large notional values, now represents a significant figure on the bottom line of a bank or corporation. Consequently, it is important that risk measurement techniques now become extremely accurate measurements of that risk.

Without sophisticated measuring and analysis systems, financial institutions would be unable to cope with the risks involved. This book describes such a system, firstly from a theoretical viewpoint and then by illustrating the theory with numerical examples.

This book sets out a logical approach to the measurement of price risk positions. Though primarily aimed at derivative dealers and end-users, the principles involved can be applied to more conventional financial instruments, such as loans and leases. For convenience, I have used the term 'institution', rather than a more cumbersome phrase such as 'dealers and end-users'.

Chapters 2 and 3 set the theoretical framework for this approach – the concept of factor sensitivity analysis. This is then applied to a number of simple individual instruments, before the analysis is extended to portfolios of instruments and multiple instruments in Chapter 5.

The use of factor sensitivity analysis in managing a portfolio of instruments is explained in Chapters 4 and 5. This uses a swap warehouse as an example, and shows how the method can be used to virtually eliminate the major risks in the warehouse. The method is then extended to cover foreign exchange options.

Chapter 6 contains a brief overview of elementary statistics, which are then applied to calculating price risk exposures. This leads to the introduction of limits to control the risks within acceptable bounds in Chapter 7. The various alternative treatments for non-linear or asymmetric risks are described and adapted to cover stress testing in Chapters 8 and 9.

Chapter 10 sets out various approaches to estimating capital requirements, both economic and regulatory.

The understanding of the risks involved in trading derivatives can no longer be confined to the traders and 'rocket scientists', but must be understood at all levels of management throughout the institution. This book is aimed at just such a wide audience. Consequently, the approach does not involve any complicated mathematics whatsoever – high school mathematics is sufficient to understand all the detail. However, those with less mathematical ability should not be deterred, as the mathematics is concentrated in specific areas which can be omitted without detracting from the overall understanding. In those cases where such mathematics occurs within the text, it has been deliberately kept brief. Although the use of more complicated mathematical formulae has been avoided, this has not deterred the author from exploring the complex ramifications behind even apparently simple approaches to measuring and managing market risk.

In 1993, the Group of Thirty in Washington published a paper entitled 'Derivatives: Practices and Principles', which listed a set of recommendations that should result in a good risk management system for derivative instruments. These were mostly aimed at dealers and end-users and covered a wide variety of topics, including valuation and market risk management, credit risk measurement and management, systems, operations and controls. There were also a number of recommendations for legislators, regulators and supervisors.

This book concentrates on market risk, so only those recommendations covering market risk will be discussed. In many cases, the author has adhered strictly to the Group of Thirty recommendations, but there are cases where the exact recommendation fails to cover the topic either completely or accurately. The reader is encouraged to read the report of the Group of Thirty and to examine where this book departs from their recommendations.

CHAPTER TWO

Market Valuation

2.1 Philosophy and Policies of Marking to Market

The fundamental purpose of marking a portfolio to market is to obtain an objective measurement of the current market value, and hence of the profit and loss, of the portfolio. Essentially this is required for the accounting books of the institution, but it also serves a number of other purposes.

The first purpose is to measure the accounting results of the individual unit, in particular calculating the profit or loss attributable to that unit. In measuring the financial performance of a unit, the profit or loss is usually compared against the budget for the unit. However, it must also be compared against the risk that the unit undertakes, to calculate a return on risk. Obviously, a higher profit figure is almost always welcome, but not if it is achieved by taking a higher degree of risk that could be regarded as excessive.

The other major purpose is to control losses, which is done by setting loss limits and comparing performance-to-date against those loss limits. If performance month-to-date is regarded as unsatisfactory, perhaps due to a significant month-to-date loss, then it may be possible to take corrective action in a timely manner, either to prevent further losses or hopefully to attempt to recover some of the loss.

The philosophy of marking to market is to simulate the orderly liquidation or hedging of a price risk position. Thus it must represent an unquestionable best-effort estimate of the price levels at which liquidation or hedging can realistically be done. Clearly if the institution has a large swap book, comprising both long and short swaps, it is not necessary to liquidate all the long swaps and all the short swaps; it is only the mismatch between the long and short positions that has to be closed out in the market place. If the entire portfolio had to be liquidated, it would have to be done at extremely low fire-sale prices, and not at realistic price levels.

The policy of marking to market requires the daily input of the present value of a portfolio, using approved sources for those prices and/or using an approved model. This frequency can be different for accounting and risk management purposes. For trading accounts, the frequency is usually daily for accounting purposes and at least daily for risk management purposes. Clearly for investment accounts held at historic cost, the marking to market for accounting purposes can be infrequent. However these must still be marked to market on at least a daily basis for risk management purposes.

In any warehouse in which there is considerable activity during the day, it is essential that changes in the value of the warehouse are estimated on a regular basis. This does not necessarily include a full mark-to-market valuation, as there are many approximations that are sufficiently accurate for risk management purposes. These will be described in detail in Section 5.2: Managing a swap portfolio.

2.2 Sound Implementation Procedures

Each institution should establish sound implementation procedures. These cover a wide range of points which must be taken into consideration in coming up with a fair price.

The type of market, commodity or instrument will influence the price. In particular, the effect of the size of the position and the market share of the institution on trading liquidity must be considered. In many instruments, the liquidity dries up completely at longer tenors, even though there is no problem at short tenors. If there are problems, then a discount may have to be considered in establishing a sound mark-to-market valuation. However, in many cases, the mid-market price is a suitable price at which to value the instrument. This will be discussed further in Chapter 5.

The responsibilities of the various interested parties need to be firmly established. Wherever possible the valuation should be made using independent external sources. Such external sources should be formally approved as a matter of policy. In any case, these prices will normally be supplied by the trader and then reviewed by an independent officer in the back-office. It is also perfectly acceptable to perform these functions in reverse – the prices being supplied by the back-office and then reviewed by the trader to ensure that there is no problem with an external source. For example, certain prices may be obtained regularly from a particular external source whose screen prices are regarded as reliable, except for the year-end valuation because the screen prices from that particular source are not updated from the week-end before Christmas until the first weekend in the New Year. The Risk Management Department and the Financial Control Department are also involved, on an ongoing basis, to ensure that the sources are reliable and the data is sound .

For liquid markets, there is very little problem in establishing a reliable external source of prices. For illiquid markets, other techniques have to be used. The only prices available may be those used in recent transactions, or prices from other units within the same institution. One method that is often used is to value the instrument using a constant spread to a known liquid market. This spread must be verified whenever possible, such as when a trade is executed by a third party in the market place or when the instrument is actually sold by the institution. Although there is no need to value an instrument after it has been sold, this provides a useful cross-check on the validity of the spread that has been used, which could be of benefit when a new trade is undertaken.

2.3 Pricing Models

Of critical importance to the valuation of most derivatives transactions is the pricing model. Clearly, a pricing model is required to value an instrument that does not have a directly-quoted market price. A pricing model is also needed, however, for those instruments that have quoted prices, in order to accurately calculate the price risk of the instrument.

Most derivative instruments need a model. Such a model could be as simple as taking the quoted price in percentage terms from a Reuters screen – such as the quoted price for US Treasuries – and then multiplying this percentage by the notional value of the transaction. However, a model as trivial as this is of no use for price risk management purposes.

A typical model for a derivative would be that applied to an interest rate swap. This involves taking the yield curve from the screen and then using that yield curve to calculate the present value of all the future cash flows of the swap. The present value concept is implicit in all pricing models – either the present value of all the known future cash flows, or the present value of all the expected future cash flows in the case of options and floating rate instruments.

The input data to such models must be carefully controlled and checked, as a model is only as good as the data it receives. If the data comes from a real-time medium, such as a Reuters screen, then it must be obtained at a consistent time each and every day. If it is then re-input manually, careful checking is essential. If input data is transferred electronically from one computer to another, then sufficient integrity checks must be incorporated into these computer systems.

The model itself must also be carefully checked. Obviously, the model must have undergone all the appropriate systems and acceptance testing that is expected of any computer program. These tests ensure that the mathematics, as given in the detailed functional specifications, is correctly implemented. In addition, it is essential that a model validation exercise be performed to ensure that the correct mathematics is specified in the detailed function specification. This validation process also ensures consistency within the institution. For example, there are a number of perfectly acceptable mathematical techniques for interpolating yields, and an institution can reasonably adopt any one of these. However, no institution should ever use one interpolation technique to value an instrument and a different interpolation technique to value the hedge. Clearly, such validation is not required for models as trivial as the US Treasuries model referred to above.

The mathematics in each of these models can be expressed in such a way that the value of the instrument is some function of the terms and conditions of the instrument and the current market value of certain market factors. It is these market factors that are covered in the following section.

2.4 Market Factors

Market factors are the independent variables that directly affect the value of an instrument, where the value of the instrument depends upon the terms and conditions of the instrument and the market factors. This somewhat circular definition is best resolved by giving examples.

2.4.1 Market Factors: price

The market factors that are 'prices' include:
    foreign exchange rates
    interest rates
    equity prices
    commodity prices
To value a foreign exchange transaction, we clearly need to know the foreign exchange rate. This market factor will appear directly in the mathematical formula for the value of the foreign exchange transaction.

In the analysis that follows, it is only the market factors that directly influence the value of an instrument that are considered. For example, the price of oil is one market factor used in calculating the value of an oil swap; it is not a market factor used in valuing a forward foreign exchange agreement for Japanese yen against the US dollar, even though that exchange rate will probably change if the price of oil changes. The price of oil does not appear in the valuation formula, so it is not considered to be a market factor for this foreign exchange transaction.

There is a vast array of market factors for interest rates. There are different interest rates in every currency; there are many different types of interest rate (or yield curve) in a given currency, such as government rates, swap rates, etc.; and there are different rates at each tenor on a given yield curve – the term structure of interest rates.

The market factors for the various instruments are given following the pricing model for each instrument in Section 2.6.

2.4.2 Market Factors: Volatility

In addition to those given above, there are many more market factors involved when option portfolios are considered. These are the 'volatilities' of all the above market factors. In order to price a foreign exchange option, the volatility of the foreign exchange rate between the two currencies is needed. In any significant portfolio of foreign exchange options, there will be a very large number of such volatilities. This is because there is a separate distinct volatility for each pair of currencies between which options are written. This is in direct contrast to the foreign exchange rates themselves.

If both the Deutschmark–Dollar (DEM/USD) and the French Franc–Dollar (FRF/USD) foreign exchange rates are known, then the French Franc–Deutschmark (FRF/DEM) rate can be deduced by division. Thus there is no need for the FRF/DEM foreign exchange rate to be treated as a separate market factor. However if the DEM/USD and the FRF/USD volatilities are known, then nothing whatsoever is known about the FRF/DEM volatility.

The volatility of the FRF/DEM foreign exchange rate is a completely separate market factor. In order to calculate it from the volatilities of DEM/USD and FRF/USD, an additional piece of information is required, namely the correlation between the two foreign exchange rates. Correlations are also specified for each pair of currencies, so the use of correlation does not reduce the number of market factors; it merely expresses them in a different form.

In considering options on interest rate instruments, there are volatilities associated with each point on each yield curve. Thus there is a term structure of volatilities analogous to the term structure of interest rates. To be precise, there are a number of different volatilities associated with each point on the yield curve, depending upon the relative values of the strike price of the option and the current spot interest rate – the so-called 'volatility smile'.

2.4.3 Market Factors: Time

Market factors have been defined as the independent variables that directly affect the value of an instrument, where the value of the instrument depends upon the terms and conditions of the instrument and the market factors. From this definition, it could be argued that time should be a market factor. It certainly does change during the life of a transaction, unlike the terms and conditions of the contract. However, because the rate of change in the remaining time-to-maturity is completely predictable, it is not regarded in the same light as the market factors which change unpredictably.

The factor sensitivity analysis, described in the following chapter, is performed for each of the market factors. A similar analysis is also done with respect to time, and is particularly important in option portfolios, but the result is not used in the limit monitoring process in the same way.

2.5 Valuation Techniques

2.5.1 Present Value

The simplest financial instrument is probably a short-term placement, in which the institution is to receive just one cash flow (principal and interest) on a given date in the future. The valuation of that placement is simply the present value of that cash flow. The whole concept of valuation is in fact based on finding the present value of a series of known cash flows. When it comes to options, this becomes the present value of a series of probable cash flows. The most basic formula in financial mathematics is the formula for the present value of a cash flow at some point in the future.

Consider a simple example in which 100 is invested at 10% for one year. Clearly, this will be worth 110 in one year – 100 of principal and 10 of interest. In this case, 100 is the present value of 110 in one year.

$$FV = PV(1 + R)$$

or $\qquad PV = FV / (1 + R)$

where $\qquad PV = 100$ is the present value

$\qquad\qquad FV = 110$ is the future value

$\qquad\qquad R = 10\%$ is the annual rate of interest.

If 100 is invested at an annual rate of 10% for two years becomes 121, because in the second year interest is earned on 110 – interest is paid at the end of the first year and is added to the principal to earn interest during the second year. In other words, the interest is compound interest rather than simple interest.

We have $\qquad PV = FV_0$

$\qquad\qquad FV_1 = FV_0(1 + R)$

$\qquad\qquad FV_2 = FV_1(1 + R)$

$\qquad\qquad\quad = FV_0(1 + R)(1 + R)$

$\qquad\qquad\quad = PV(1 + R)^2$

where $\qquad PV = 100$ is the present value

$\qquad\qquad FV = 121$ is the future value

$\qquad\qquad R = 10\%$ is the annual rate of interest.

The general case is:

$$FV = PV(1+R)^T$$

or $$PV = FV / (1+R)^T$$

PV is the present value

FV is the future value

R is the annual rate of interest

T is the time in years.

That is to say, the future cash flow is divided by one plus the interest rate raised to the power of the time to obtain the present value.

Almost all valuation models are based on this formula. It should be noted that in the examples given above, the tenors are exact numbers of years and the interest rate is quoted on an annual basis. The formula is identical in other cases, where the tenor is an exact multiple of the period for which the interest rate applies, though in this case R becomes the interest rate per period and T becomes the number of periods. The most common example is the use of semi-annual interest instruments in which interest is paid every six months.

When the tenor is not a complete number of periods, then assumptions have to be made about the interest that will be earned during the stub period. For example, if the tenor of an interest-bearing instrument is five years and two months, then interest will usually be paid after two months and then at regular intervals thereafter: this initial two-month period is known as the 'stub period'. Usually, the stub period is the first period, though there are cases where it is the last period. There are two different approaches to this problem in use in the financial community.

Consider the case of the tenor being less than one year. The first approach is to use the formula given above for compound interest, namely $PV = FV / (1 + R)^T$, with a fractional value of T. However, market practice is to use the formula for simple interest, namely $PV = FV / (1 + RT)$. Conceptually, there are no strong arguments in favour of either formula, but, as the simple interest method has become market practice, it is the formula that must be used.

Money market rates are quoted on the assumption that the simple interest formulae will be used. In many countries, the money market rate is quoted on a different basis to longer term rates. This will be discussed in Section 2.5.3.

When the tenor is greater than 12 months, the problem referred to above in handling the interest for the stub period also arises. In this case, it is far more common to use the formula for compound interest, namely $PV = FV / (1 + R)^T$, where T is not an integer. For example, if the cash flow is 2.75 years away, the formula could be:

$$PV = FV / (1 + R)^{2.75}$$

where R is the 2.75 year rate.

Alternatively the formula could apply simple interest to the stub period:

$$PV = FV / \left[(1+R)^2 (1+0.75R) \right]$$

These formulae are entirely analogous to the formulae that were described for tenors of less than one year.

2.5.2 Compounding Frequency

The above formula assumes an annual compounding frequency. It is worth examining what happens when the compounding frequency is more frequent than annual .

For example, let us consider a one-year investment of 100 at a semi-annual rate of 10% per annum. In this case, there are two periods to consider. During the first six-month period, the principal of 100 earns interest of 5, which is then added to the principal to obtain 105. During the second six-month period, the interest earned is 5.25, because it is calculated on a principal balance of 105, rather than 100. The future value of the 100 is 110.25. This could have been obtained by using the formula:

$$FV = PV(1 + R / N)^N$$

where $R / 2 = 5\%$ is the interest rate per period

$N = 2$ is the number of periods.

Thus, we have established that the future value is the present value times $(1 + R)^N$, where R is the interest rate per period and N is the number of periods. Consider a cash flow that will occur in exactly one year.

If the rate is quoted annually then the formula is simply:

$$FV = PV(1 + R).$$

If the rate is quoted semi-annually, then the formula will be:

$$FV = PV(1 + R / 2)^2.$$

If the rate is quoted monthly, then the formula will be:

$$FV = PV(1 + R / 12)^{12}.$$

The effective annual rate (R_a) for a compounding frequency of N periods per annum is given by:

$$PV(1 + R_a) = PV(1 + R_n / N)^N$$

or

$$R_a = (1 + R_n / N)^N - 1.$$

The effect of increasing the compounding frequency is shown in Table 2.1, which shows the true effective annual rate for a quoted 8% rate which is then compounded at the various frequencies.

As the compounding frequency increases, the effective annual rate does continue to increase. However, once the compounding is more frequent than daily, the differences are in the fifth significant figure or even lower. The effective annual rate approaches a limit. This can be clearly seen in the graph in Figure 2.1, in which the effective annual rate is plotted against the compounding frequency. Note that the frequency scale is not linear in this graph.

In mathematical terms, this limit is given by:

$$\operatorname*{Limit}_{N \to \infty}(1 + R / N)^N = e^R$$

Table 2.1 Annual Percentage Rates

Compounding	Effective rate (%)
Annual	8.000
Semi-annual	8.160
Quarterly	8.243
Monthly	8.300
Weekly	8.322
Daily	8.328
Hourly	8.328
Minute	8.328
Second	8.328
Continuous	8.328

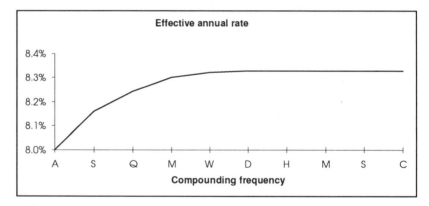

Figure 2.1 Effective annual rate

This limit is in fact the exponential function of the rate, R. This is a very useful result, as it brings us into the mathematics of exponential functions, which is a very well-known area of mathematics. So much so, that most financial textbooks immediately move into continuous compounded rates, especially when dealing with options.

Discrete annual rates can be simply converted into continuous compounding or exponential rates. This is done by finding the continuous compounding rate R_c whose exponential is equal to $(1 + R_a)$, where R_a is the annual rate. In symbols:

$$1 + R_a = e^{R_c}.$$

By taking the natural logarithm of both sides, we find that the continuous compounding rate is the natural log of (one plus the annual rate):

$$R_c = \ln(1 + R_a).$$

This is asking a different question to the one outlined previously. In this case, we are not asking what effective rate is equivalent to a quoted continuous compounding rate, but rather what continuous compounding rate is equivalent to a given quoted effective annual rate.

If the effective annual rate is 8%, expressed as 0.08, then the natural log of 1.08 is 0.076961. So a 7.696% continuous compounding rate for one year will give exactly the same return as an 8% annual rate. As a second example, 9.53% is the equivalent continuous compounding rate to a 10% annual rate.

2.5.3 Discount Factors

Let us now concentrate on the discount factors that are used to present value future cash flows.

We have established that:

$$FV = PV(1 + R)^T$$

and that

$$PV = FV / (1 + R)^T = D * FV.$$

The discount factor D is simply the multiplicative factor required to convert a future value into a present value.

When interest rates are quoted annually, this becomes:

$$D = (1 + R_a)^{-T}.$$

When interest rates are continuous compounding rates, this becomes:

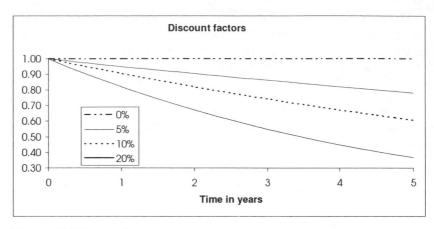

Figure 2.2 Discount factors

$$D = e^{-RT}$$

where R_a is the effective annual rate

               R is the continuous compounding rate

               T is the time in years.

The discount factors for different values of the continuous compounding rate are shown in Figure 2.2.

The above derivation assumes that the quoted interest rate represents the exact rate for the exact period, such as an annual period. In many countries, the money market quotes interest rates on an actual over 360 basis: that is, the rate is multiplied by the actual number of days in the period divided by 360. This means that the discount factor formula for periods of up to one year has to be modified slightly to read:

$$D = 1 / (1 + R\,d\,/\,360)$$

where R is the quoted annual money market rate

and d is the exact number of days.

Note that this results in a higher interest payment than is

implied by the quoted rate. For example, on a principal of 1,000,000, a 10% bond basis rate results in a payment of 100,000, whereas a 10% annual money market rate results in a payment of 101,388.89 in a 365-day year.

On the other hand, for longer tenor instruments, rates are usually quoted on a bond basis. For instruments with regular annual payments, the interest payments are calculated using the quoted rate. For instruments with regular semi-annual payments, the interest payments are usually calculated using exactly half the quoted rate every six months, regardless of how many days there are in each six-month period. However, there are some cases where the amount paid depends upon the actual number of days in the period.

2.5.4 Bond Valuation

The formulae given in the preceding sections dealt with the calculation of the present value of a single future cash flow. It is also very useful to be able to calculate the present value of a stream of regular equal cash flows. Typically this occurs in a bond, where the stream of cash flows represents the regular interest payments, though there is also a single payment at maturity representing the return of the principal.

Let us consider a fixed rate bond, principal amount P, which pays an annual coupon C for N years. This gives a series of $(N–1)$ annual cash flows of amount PC followed by one cash flow of $(P + PC)$ in year N.

Using the formula already established for the discount factors, the present value of each cash flow can be evaluated. The present value of the fixed rate bond is then the sum of the individual present values of these cash flows.

$$V = PC(1+R)^{-1} + PC(1+R)^{-2} + ...$$
$$+ PC(1+R)^{-N+1} + PC(1+R)^{-N} + P(1+R)^{-N}.$$

This may appear to be a rather difficult formula to handle as it involves so many terms. However, all the terms (except the final

one) form a geometric series, and there is a relatively simple formula for the sum of a geometric series. As a result, the valuation
can be expressed by the following formula:

$$V = PC\left(1-(1+R)^{-N}\right)/R + P(1+R)^{-N}$$

where V is the present value of the bond
             P is the principal of the bond
             C is the coupon rate of the bond
             N is the number of periods
             R is the market interest rate per period.

This formula has two terms: the first term is the sum of the
present values of all the coupon payments, and the second term
is the present value of the final payment of principal at maturity.

When a fixed rate bond is issued with a coupon equal to the
current market yield, it is issued at par, which means that its value
is equal to the principal. Thus one important check on the above
valuation is to set the coupon (C) equal to the market rate (R).
When this is done, it can be seen that many of the terms cancel,
and the formula reduces to $V = P$ as expected.

The above discussion has been phrased in present value terminology; namely, using a known market rate to obtain the
present value of the instrument. The same formula can, of course,
be used to calculate the unknown yield-to-maturity when the
market price of the bond is known. This yield cannot be expressed
directly as a formula, but can be found by using iterative search
techniques on the above formula. One common technique is the
Newton-Raphson method, using the known coupon as the starting value for the iteration.

In this chapter all the cash flows of an instrument have been
discounted at the same interest rate to obtain the present value of
the instrument. The more complex method using zero coupon
discount factors will be described in detail in Section 4.1.

2.6 Simple Valuation Models

Let us now apply these valuation techniques to a range of different products, thereby deriving some simple pricing models. The more complex pricing models will be discussed in detail in a later chapter.

2.6.1 Spot Foreign Exchange Transactions

The valuation formula for a spot foreign exchange transaction to or from the base currency of the institution is given by:

$$V = P_f\ FX + P_d$$

where P_f is the amount of the foreign currency

         P_d is the amount in the domestic currency

       FX is the spot foreign exchange rate expressed

            as the amount of local currency per unit of

            foreign currency.

The formula simply converts the amount in the foreign currency into the base currency by multiplying by the foreign exchange rate, and then adds the amount in the base currency. These two amounts are signed and must have opposite signs – positive for a cash inflow and negative for a cash outflow. Thus the same formula covers both the purchase and the sale of the foreign currency by setting the signs appropriately.

Clearly the two amounts are terms and conditions of the transaction, whereas the foreign exchange rate (FX) is a market factor which can change between the time at which the transaction is agreed and the time of settlement, which is usually two working days later. The exact date is, of course, also a term of the contract.

If the foreign exchange contract results in the exchange of two currencies, neither of which is the base currency of the institution, then the formula needs a simple modification to handle such a cross-rate transaction. The formula is as follows:

$$V = P_1 \, FX_1 + P_2 \, FX_2$$

where P_1 is the amount of the first foreign currency

FX_1 is the spot foreign exchange rate of currency 1

P_2 is the amount of the second foreign currency

FX_2 is the spot foreign exchange rate of currency 2.

Both foreign exchange rates are expressed as the amount of base currency per unit of foreign currency. The formula simply converts each foreign currency into the base currency and then adds them together.

Analysing this valuation formula, it is clear that there are now two market factors required for the valuation of this transaction, namely the two foreign exchange rates, FX_1 and FX_2.

2.6.2 Fixed Interest Instruments

There is a wide variety of fixed interest instruments, but the valuation of each of them depends upon simple present value concepts discussed earlier in this chapter.

The formula for the value of a fixed rate bond, as derived in Section 2.5.4 is:

$$V = PC\left(1 - (1+R)^{-N}\right)/R + P(1+R)^{-N}$$

where V is the present value of the bond

P is the principal of the bond

C is the coupon rate of the bond

N is the number of periods

R is the market interest rate per period.

Analysing this valuation formula, it is clear that there is only one market factor required for the valuation of this transaction, namely the market interest rate R.

2.6.3 Forward Foreign Exchange Transactions

The pricing model for a forward foreign exchange transaction is readily obtained by adding a present value process to the model for a spot foreign exchange transaction.

The value of a spot foreign exchange transaction is given by:

$$V = P_1 \, FX_1 + P_2 \, FX_2$$

The value of a forward foreign exchange transaction is therefore given by:

$$V = P_1 \, FX_1 (1 + R_1)^{-T} + P_2 \, FX_2 (1 + R_2)^{-T}$$

where P_1 is the amount of the first foreign currency

FX_1 is the spot foreign exchange rate of currency 1

R_1 is the interest rate in the first currency

P_2 is the amount of the second foreign currency

FX_2 is the spot foreign exchange rate of currency 2

R_2 is the interest rate in the second currency

T is the tenor of the transaction in years.

In this formula, the amount in the first currency P_1 is present valued using the interest rate in the first currency R_1, and then converted to the base currency by multiplying by the foreign exchange rate FX_1, expressed in units of the base currency per unit of the foreign currency. The present value of the amount in the second currency P_2 is present valued using the interest rate in the second currency R_2, and then converted to the base currency by multiplying by the exchange rate FX_2, expressed in units of the base currency per unit of the foreign currency. These are then added to obtain the value of the transaction, remembering that the values P_1 and P_2 will have opposite signs.

Analysing this valuation formula, it is clear that there are four market factors required for the valuation of this transaction, namely the foreign exchange rates FX_1 and FX_2, the interest rate in the first currency R_1, and the interest rate in the second currency R_2.

If the second currency is the base currency, then the foreign exchange rate FX_2 becomes unity, and the interest rate R_2 is the domestic interest rate. This simplifies the formula a little, and it can then be written as:

$$V = P_f\, FX \left(1 + R_f\right)^{-T} + P_d \left(1 + R_d\right)^{-T}$$

where the subscript f refers to the foreign currency and the subscript d refers to the domestic currency.

Analysing this valuation formula, it is clear that there are now only three market factors required for the valuation of this transaction, namely the foreign exchange rate FX, the foreign interest rate R_f, and the domestic interest rate R_d.

CHAPTER THREE

Simple Factor Sensitivity Analysis

3.1 Definition of Factor Sensitivity

The value of a financial instrument depends upon the terms and conditions of the contract and the current value of the relevant market factors. Not only is it useful to know those market factors, but it is also of considerable interest to know exactly how the value of that instrument could change for a given change in the market factors.

The **factor sensitivity** of a position is defined as the change in the value of the position caused by a unit shift in a given market factor. Thus a position has as many factor sensitivities as there are underlying market factors. The unit shift must be defined separately for each market factor.

A typical set of unit shifts would be:

Interest rates	+ 1 basis point absolute
Prices (including FX)	+ 1 % relative
Volatilities	+ 1 basis point absolute.

The calculation of the factor sensitivity of a spot foreign exchange position is obtained by valuing the position using the current spot foreign exchange rate, valuing the position using the current spot foreign exchange rate increased by 1%, and then calculating the resultant change in value by subtracting the initial valuation from the final valuation.

The calculation of the factor sensitivity of a bond is obtained by valuing the bond using the current interest rate, valuing the bond using the current interest rate increased by 1 basis point, and then calculating the resultant change in value by subtracting the initial valuation from the final valuation.

An alternative mathematical expression can be derived from an examination of the definition of factor sensitivity, namely:

Factor Sensitivity = Change in value / Change in market factor

$$FS = \Delta V / \Delta y$$

If we plot a graph of the value of a position (V) against the value of the underlying market factor (y), the change in value for a unit change in the market factor is simply the slope of the graph, when expressed in the appropriate units. This can be approximated by the expression, $\Delta V / \Delta y$. More accurately, this is the first derivative of the value with respect to the market factor (dV/dy), which in many cases can be derived analytically using differential calculus to obtain the instantaneous rate of change in value. Examples of these alternative definitions will be included as the various instruments are examined in turn.

The method of calculating factor sensitivity is best illustrated with a few simple examples. These examples also serve to illustrate a number of other points concerning factor sensitivity, which are needed for more complex analyses.

3.2 Spot Foreign Exchange Transactions

3.2.1 Pricing Model

The valuation formula for a spot foreign exchange transaction to or from the base currency of the institution, as derived in Section 2.6.1, is:

$$V = P_f \ FX + P_d$$

where P_f is the amount in the foreign currency

P_d is the amount on the domestic currency

FX is the spot foreign exchange rate, expressed as the amount of local currency per unit of foreign currency.

The valuation formula for a spot foreign exchange transaction that results in the exchange of two currencies, neither of which is the base currency of the institution, as derived in Section 2.6.1, is:

$$V = P_1 FX_1 + P_2 FX_2$$

where P_1 is the amount in the first foreign currency

   FX_1 is the spot foreign exchange rate of currency 1

   P_2 is the amount in the second foreign currency

   FX_2 is the spot foreign exchange rate of currency 2.

Both foreign exchange rates are expressed as the amount of local currency per unit of foreign currency.

3.2.2 Example Involving the Base Currency

The examples in this section assume that sterling is the base currency of the institution and that all transactions are dealt at the current mid-market foreign exchange rates, which are:

DEM / GBP= 2.5

USD / GBP = 1.5

Note that these foreign exchange rates are quoted on a different basis to that required in the valuation formula. For a British institution, these quotes are in terms of foreign currency per unit of base currency, instead of units of base currency per unit of foreign currency. Rather than quoting these rates in an unconventional manner, it is usually simpler to require division by the foreign exchange rate instead of multiplication. However, as we shall see, this creates a number of minor problems.

The factor sensitivities of a spot foreign exchange contract could now be calculated using the first formula in Section 3.2.1. However, let us first look at an example without using any valuation formulae.

Let us assume that a British institution enters into a spot foreign exchange contract to purchase DEM 2,500,000 in exchange for GBP 1,000,000. At the current spot rate of 2.5, the mark-to-market value of this spot contract is zero. After two working days have elapsed, the normal settlement period for a spot contract, the institution will receive DEM 2,500,000, which is worth GBP 1,000,000, and will pay away GBP 1,000,000, giving a net mark-to-market value of zero. However, if the Deutschmark were suddenly to appreciate by 1% against the pound sterling, then the mark-to-market value of this contract would change. Although the institution still expects to receive DEM 2,500,000, this is now worth 1% more in terms of pounds, namely GBP 1,010,000. The new mark-to-market value of the contract is now GBP 10,000, where previously it had been zero. Thus the factor sensitivity, the change in value for a 1% increase in the foreign exchange rate, is GBP 10,000.

Next, let us assume that the British institution enters into a spot foreign exchange contract to sell DEM 2,500,000 in exchange for GBP 1,000,000. The current mark-to-market value of this spot contract is also zero. The institution will pay away DEM 2,500,000, which is worth GBP 1,000,000, and will receive GBP 1,000,000, giving a net mark-to-market value of zero. If the Deutschmark were to suddenly appreciate by 1%, then the mark-to-market value of this contract would change. Although the institution still expects to pay away DEM 2,500,000, this is now worth 1% more in terms of pounds, namely GBP 1,010,000. The new mark-to-market value of the contract is now GBP (10,000) – a negative number – where previously it had been zero. This is the extra amount, in terms of its base currency, that the institution now has to pay away, so it has a negative sign. Thus the factor sensitivity, the change in value for a 1% increase in the foreign exchange rate, is GBP (10,000).

Although the magnitude of the factor sensitivity shows exactly how sensitive the bottom line is to a 1% change in the value of the foreign currency, the sign of the factor sensitivity is also important. If the institution executed both the above contracts, perhaps with different counterparties, it would have no price risk whatsoever. The cash inflows and outflows in both GBP and DEM are exactly equal and opposite, so there is no net cash flow in either currency. This exact matching is also shown by the fact that the positive factor sensitivity 10,000 is exactly offset by the negative factor sensitivity (10,000) – the total factor sensitivity to a 1% change in the value of the foreign currency is zero.

Let us now calculate the factor sensitivities for the above transactions using the valuation formula for a spot foreign exchange transaction involving the base currency of the institution:

$$V = P_f\ FX + P_d$$

where P_f is the amount in the foreign currency

P_d is the amount in the domestic currency

FX is the spot foreign exchange rate, expressed as the number of units of base currency per unit of foreign currency.

Applying this valuation formula to the first transaction (buying DEM), we have:

$$V_0 - 2,500,000 * 0.4 - 1,000,000 = \quad GBP\ 0$$
$$V_1 - 2,500,000 * 0.404 - 1,000,000 = GBP\ 10,000$$

With this method of expressing foreign exchange rates, the expected answer is obtained when the foreign exchange rate is multiplied by 1.01, which represents a 1% appreciation of the foreign currency.

If we use the standard representation of the foreign exchange rate, and apply this valuation formula to the first transaction (buying DEM) and remember to divide by the exchange rate, rather than multiplying by the exchange rate, we have:

$$V_0 = 2,500,000 / 2.5 - 1,000,000 = GBP\ 0$$

If the DEM appreciates against the pound by 1%, then the quoted foreign exchange rate will be lower. At first sight, it would seem logical to use 2.475, as this is 99% of the initial foreign exchange rate of 2.5. However, if 2.475 is substituted into the above formula, we obtain:

$$V_1 = 2,500,000 / 2.475 - 1,000,000 = GBP\ 10,101$$

This is not the expected answer that was derived earlier without using the formula, nor is it the answer obtained using the non-standard representation of the foreign exchange rate. The reason for this is that the foreign exchange rate should not have been changed by multiplying by 0.99, but by dividing by 1.01. This gives a new foreign exchange rate of 2.475248. This is equivalent to multiplying by 1.01 when the foreign exchange rate is expressed as the number of units of base currency per unit of foreign currency: in this example, 0.400 is the inverse of 2.5 and 0.404 is the inverse of 2.475248. If this value is substituted into the formula, then we obtain:

$$V_1 2,500,000 / 2.475248 - 1,000,000 = \text{GBP } 10,000$$

It is worth repeating the calculation for a 1% depreciation of DEM against GBP. To produce an equivalent change in the foreign exchange rate for a depreciation to that used for an appreciation, the new exchange rate is obtained by dividing by 0.99. In this case the new exchange rate will be 2.5/1.01 or 2.525253. This is equivalent to using a foreign exchange rate of 0.396, when the exchange rate is expressed in units of base currency per unit of foreign currency. Substituting this into the equation, we have:

$$V_1 = 2,500,000 / 2.525253 - 1,000,000 = \text{GBP } (10,000)$$

Alternatively:

$$V_1 = 2,500,000 * 0.396 - 1,000,000 = \text{GBP } (10,000)$$

This shows that the change in value due to a 1% decrease in the foreign exchange rate is exactly an equal and opposite amount to the change in value due to a 1% increase in the foreign exchange rate. However, in the above analysis the foreign exchange rates used for a depreciation, for the base case and for an appreciation are 0.396, 0.400 and 0.404 respectively, using the non-standard representation. The change in the foreign exchange rate is either −0.004 or +0.004, so these are exactly equal and opposite changes in the exchange rate. When the exchange rate is quoted using the standard representation, the foreign exchange rates used for a depreciation, for the base case and for an appreciation are

2.525253, 2.5 and 2.475248 respectively. The change in the foreign exchange rate is either –0.024752 or +0.025253, so these are not exactly equal and opposite changes in the exchange rate.

When the standard representation is used and equal changes are made, a certain asymmetry appears. This asymmetry is illustrated in Figure 3.1, which shows the value of the above foreign exchange transaction for a wide range of foreign exchange rates, namely from 2.25 to 2.75. The valuation is shown as a continuous line and is a gentle curve, and not a straight line. A straight line, shown as a dotted line, has been drawn to indicate just how close the valuation curve is to being a straight line over reasonable changes in the standard foreign exchange rate. However, as we will see in later chapters, such asymmetry only becomes a major problem when we start examining options.

The factor sensitivity of the transaction is the change in value for a unit change in the market factor. Graphically, this is simply the slope of the graph, and is therefore the slope of the straight line above. The fact that the valuation does not depart significantly from the straight line is an indication that the factor sensitivity itself is fairly insensitive to the market rates used in its calculation. If the factor sensitivity were calculated using 2.475 instead of 2.5, the resultant factor sensitivity would be a very similar number:

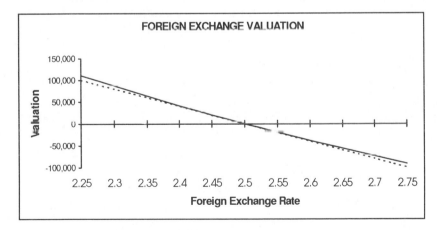

Figure 3.1   Foreign exchange valuation

$$V_1 = 2{,}500{,}000 / 2.475 - 1{,}000{,}000 \qquad = \text{GBP } 10{,}101$$
$$V_2 = 2{,}500{,}000 / 2.475 / 1.01 - 1{,}000{,}000 = \text{GBP } 20{,}202$$
$$FS = V_2 - V_1$$
$$= 20{,}202 - 10{,}101$$
$$= 10{,}101.$$

The factor sensitivity has changed from 10,000 to 10,101 using a foreign exchange that is in error by 1%. This stability is a useful property of factor sensitivity analysis, and applies to both foreign exchange and interest rate portfolios.

The factor sensitivity itself is plotted against the foreign exchange rate in the graph in Figure 3.2. It can be seen that the factor sensitivity changes with the underlying exchange rate in an almost linear manner.

When the exchange rate is quoted per unit of foreign currency, the change in the factor sensitivity is an exact linear function of the foreign exchange rate. In fact, the slight asymmetry comes from the use of the reciprocal of the exchange rate rather than from any underlying asymmetries in the factor sensitivity calculation.

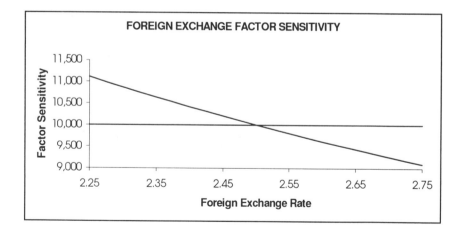

Figure 3.2   Foreign exchange factor sensitivity

3.2.3 Example of Foreign Exchange Cross

We have established that the appreciation of a foreign currency requires either a multiplication or a division by 1.01, and the depreciation of a foreign currency requires either a multiplication or a division by 0.99. This was necessary to ensure that the changes in value had the same magnitude for both the appreciation and the depreciation. In order to preserve this same symmetry in foreign exchange crosses, the symmetry of the cross-rate has to be abandoned. Foreign exchange crosses are transactions in which neither of the currencies is the base currency of the institution, for example as a DEM/USD transaction executed by a British institution.

The cross-rate for DEM/USD can be calculated by dividing (DEM/GBP) by (USD/GBP), which is DEM 2.5 / USD 1.5 = 1.666667 DEM/USD. If the DEM appreciates by 1% against the USD, the cross-rate will become 1.666667 / 1.01 = 1.650165. However, different cross-rates are obtained by allowing one currency to appreciate and allowing the other currency to depreciate.

If the DEM appreciates 1% against the GBP, the new cross-rate can be calculated:

$$DEM / GBP = 2.5 / 1.01 \quad = 2.475248$$
$$DEM / USD - 2.475248 / 1.5 = 1.650165$$

If the USD depreciates 1% against the GBP, the new cross-rate can be calculated:

$$USD / GBP - 1.5 / 0.99 \quad = 1.515152$$
$$DEM / USD = 2.5 / 1.515152 = 1.65$$

As can be seen, the cross-rate is different under the two scenarios.

The factor sensitivities of a cross-rate transaction can now be calculated using the valuation formula given in Section 3.2.1:

$$V = \quad P_1\ FX_1 + P_2\ FX_2$$

where P_1 is the amount in the first foreign currency

          FX_1 is the spot foreign exchange rate of currency 1

          P_2 is the amount in the second foreign currency

          FX_2 is the spot foreign exchange rate of currency 2.

Let us take the transaction to sell DEM 2,500,000 and buy USD 1,500,000, executed by a British institution. The initial valuation of this transaction is:

$$V_0 = 2{,}500{,}000\ /\ 2.5 - 1{,}500{,}000\ /\ 1.5 = \text{ GBP } 0$$

This contract will increase in value if the DEM appreciates by 1% against the USD. Let us examine the two cases referred to above, namely the DEM appreciates by 1% against the GBP and the USD depreciates by 1% against the GBP.

$$V_1 = 2{,}500{,}000\ /\ 2.475248 - 1{,}500{,}000\ /\ 1.5 = \text{ GBP } 10{,}000$$
$$V_2 = 2{,}500{,}000\ /\ 2.5 - 1{,}500{,}000\ /\ 1.515152 = \text{ GBP } 10{,}000$$

In both cases, the factor sensitivities are identical, even though the cross-rates are slightly different. This is another reason why appreciation uses the parameter 1.01 and depreciation uses the parameter 0.99, where the parameter is used to either multiply or divide the quoted rate, depending upon which way the rate is actually quoted.

3.2.4 Mathematical Derivation

The value of a foreign exchange transaction is given by:

$$V = P_1\ FX_1 + P_2\ FX_2$$

where the foreign exchange rates are expressed in units of base currency per unit of foreign currency.

This formula is extremely simple to differentiate, and the results are:

$$dV / dFX_1 = P_1$$
$$dV / dFX_2 = P_2$$

Thus the rate of change in value of an FX transaction is simply the value of the principal amount. This is for a change of 100%, so the factor sensitivity – the change for a 1% change – is 1% of the principal.

3.3 Fixed Interest Instruments

3.3.1 Pricing Model

There is a wide variety of fixed interest instruments, so let us first consider fixed rate bonds.

The cash flow from a one-year fixed rate bond, principal amount P, which pays an annual coupon C after one year is in fact a single cash flow at maturity, given by:

$$F = P(1 + C)$$

The present value of this future cash flow is given by:

$$V = F / (1 + R)$$

The valuation of a fixed rate bond, principal amount P, which pays an annual coupon C for N years is given by the formula:

$$V = PC\left(1 - (1 + R)^{-N}\right) / R + P(1 + R)^{-N}$$

where P is the principal of the bond

         C is the coupon per period

         N is the number of periods

         R is the market interest rate per period.

Analysing this valuation formula, it can be seen that there is only one market factor, namely the market interest rate per period (R). The other variables in the formula are all terms and conditions of the bond, which do not change with the market.

3.3.2 Examples of Fixed Rate Bonds

The factor sensitivity of a bond is calculated by valuing the bond using the current market interest rate (R) and then using the current market interest rate increased by one basis point $(R+0.0001)$. The difference between these two valuations, obtained by subtracting the initial valuation from the final valuation, is the factor sensitivity.

If an institution has bought a bond, then it is 'long' the bond – it is in the books of the institution as a positive asset. The institution will receive the coupon payments. If market rates increase, then the value of these fixed coupons will diminish, and the value of the bond will fall, which means that the factor sensitivity is a negative number.

If an institution has sold or issued a bond, then it is 'short' the bond – it is in the books of the institution as a (negative) liability. The institution will pay the coupon payments. If market rates increase, then the value of these fixed coupons will diminish, and the value of the bond will fall. However, this means that the bond has a smaller negative value, which is equivalent to an increase in value, so the factor sensitivity is a positive number.

Let us first take as an example a one-year bond which will pay an annual coupon of 8% at the end of the year in an 8% rate environment. The factor sensitivity of this bond is obtained by first valuing the bond at 8%, then valuing the bond at 8.01%, and then calculating the change in value by subtracting the initial valuation from the final valuation.

The formula for valuing a single cash flow was given in Section 2.5.1 as $V = F / (1 + R\,T)$ or alternatively $V = F / (1 + R)^T$.

In this instance, time T is equal to 1, so the two formulae give the same result. The cash flow F is equal to 1,080,000, which consists of the principal of 1,000,000 and 80,000 of interest. Applying this formula, we have:

$$V_0 = 1,080,000 / 1.08 \quad = 1,000,000.00$$
$$V_1 = 1,080,000 / 1.0801 = \quad 999,907.42$$
$$\text{Change in value} \quad = \quad (92.58)$$

Table 3.1 Factor sensitivity calculation

Time (years)	Cash flow	PV @ 8.00%	PV @ 8.01%
1	80,000	74,074.07	74,067.22
2	80,000	68,587.11	68,574.41
3	80,000	63,506.58	63,488.94
4	80,000	58,802.39	58,780.61
5	1,080,000	735,029.85	734,689.66
Total		1,000,000.00	999,600.84

The factor sensitivity of this bond, which equals the change in value, is also negative 92.58.

Let us extend this analysis to a bond with multiple cash flows, rather than a single cash flow. Consider a five-year bond which will pay an annual coupon of 8% at the end of each year in an 8% rate environment. This bond has five cash flows, and the present value of the bond can be obtained either by using the complex formula in Section 3.3.1, or by simply calculating the present value of each of the cash flows and summing them. The factor sensitivity of this bond is obtained by first valuing the bond at 8%, then valuing the bond at 8.01%, and then calculating the change in value. This is shown in Table 3.1.

By applying the complex formula, we would have derived the same result:

$$V_0 = 1,000,000.00$$
$$V_1 = 999,600.84$$
$$\text{Change in value} = (399.16)$$

Therefore, the factor sensitivity of this bond is negative 399.16.

The above method of calculating factor sensitivity can be applied to bonds of many different tenors, and the results are as shown in Table 3.2. These factor sensitivities have all been calculated for bonds with a principal of 1,000,000 with annual 8% coupons in an 8% rate environment. The factor sensitivity is positive for short bond positions and negative for long bond positions.

Table 3.2 Factor sensitivity of bonds

Tenor (years)	Factor sensitivity
1	93
2	178
3	258
4	331
5	399
7	520
10	671
15	855
20	981
30	1,125

This table shows that the factor sensitivity of the bond does not rise linearly with the tenor of the bond, but increases at a steadily decreasing rate. This can be seen more clearly in the graph in Figure 3.3. Eventually, the graph becomes asymptotic at a value of 1,248. This occurs when the principal repayment is sufficiently far in the future that its present value is negligible. The level at which this happens clearly depends upon the coupon rate on the bond, which is also assumed to be the current market rate.

It is important to examine the asymmetry, or non-linearity, of

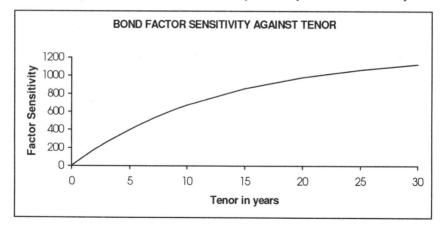

Figure 3.3   Bond factor sensitivity against tenor

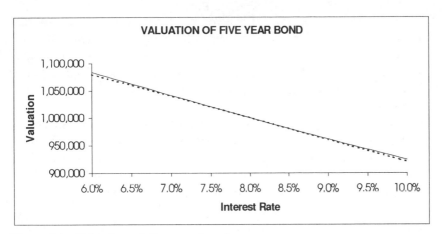

Figure 3.4   Valuation of five-year bond

the valuation of a fixed rate bond. Again this can be done graphically, and is illustrated in Figure 3.4, which shows the value of a five-year 8% 1,000,000 bond for a very wide range of interest rates, namely from 6% to 10%. In the graph, the valuation is shown as a continuous gentle curve. The dotted line is exactly a straight line, which shows just how close the valuation curve is to being a straight line over reasonable changes in interest rates. The slope of this straight line is also the factor sensitivity of the bond.

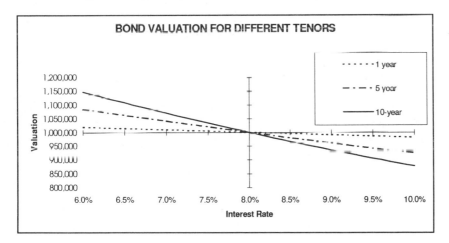

Figure 3.5   Bond valuation for different tenors

The valuation of a bond is almost a linear function of interest rates, as indicated by the very gentle curve. This near-linearity means that the factor sensitivity itself is very insensitive to changes in interest rates. This linearity applies over a wider band of potential changes in interest rates than it does in the case of foreign exchange rates.

The graph in Figure 3.5 shows the valuation of bonds of three different tenors over the same wide range of interest rates.

The 10-year bond has the steepest slope because it has the highest factor sensitivity, and the one year bond the shallowest slope because it has the lowest factor sensitivity. A secondary effect that should be noted is that the graph of the longer tenor bond has slightly more curvature than the shorter tenor bonds. However, the difference does not usually cause any significant problems.

The factor sensitivity of a five-year bond is plotted against the interest rate in the graph in Figure 3.6. The factor sensitivity changes by 10% from 400 to 360 when the interest rate changes from 8% to 10% – a fairly large change in interest rates: a 25% increase in interest rates has resulted in a 10% decrease in factor sensitivity.

This insensitivity leads to a very important conclusion, namely that the factor sensitivity does not have to be calculated using the

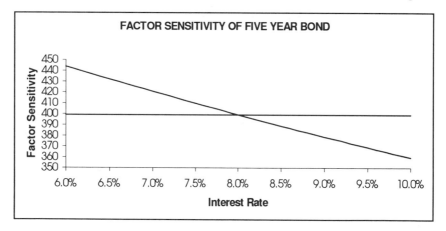

Figure 3.6   Factor sensitivity of five-year bond

exact market rates in order to obtain a sufficiently accurate result. Thus if the factor sensitivity were to be calculated using a given set of market rates, and these rates were then to change by 10 or 20 basis points, the factor sensitivities would hardly change at all. This has important practical ramifications when it comes to considering the systems that need to be implemented. For example, in obtaining end-of-day market rates for overnight batch runs, it will make very little difference to the factor sensitivities if the 5 p.m. rates are used instead of the 6 p.m. rates.

3.3.3 Mathematical Derivation

The present value of a single cash flow F at time T, which is N periods into the future, is given by the following formula:

$$V = F(1+R)^{-N}$$

where V is the present value of the bond

F is the cash flow

N is the number of periods

R is the market interest rate per period.

The change in value for a given change in the market rate can be obtained by differentiating V with respect to the rate R.

$$dV / dR = (-N)F(1+R)^{-N-1}$$
$$= (-N)F(1+R)^{N} / (1+R)$$
$$= (-N)V / (1+R)$$

As will be seen in Section 3.7, this is also the formula for the modified duration of the cash flow. Thus the concept of factor sensitivity for interest rate instruments is based on a well-tried methodology, namely duration analysis. This is discussed in more detail in Section 3.7.

The valuation of a fixed rate bond, principal amount P, which pays an annual coupon C for N years is given by the formula:

$$V = PC\left(1-(1+R)^{-N}\right)/R + P(1+R)^{-N}$$

where V is the present value of the bond

         P is the principal of the bond

         C is the coupon per period

         N is the number of periods

         R is the market interest rate per period.

This expression, which includes the sum of the geometric progression, is a little more difficult to differentiate in this form, and the result is not a simple expression. Consequently, it is simpler to differentiate the expression for the present value of each of the constituent cash flows, using the formula given above.

3.4 Forward Foreign Exchange Instruments

3.4.1 Pricing Model

The value of a forward foreign exchange transaction is given by:

$$V = P_1\, FX_1(1+R_1)^{-T} + P_2\, FX_2(1+R_2)^{-T}$$

where P_1 is the amount in the first foreign currency

         FX_1 is the spot foreign exchange rate of currency 1

         R_1 is the annual interest rate in the first currency

         P_2 is the amount in the second foreign currency

         FX_2 is the spot foreign exchange rate of currency 2

         R_2 is the annual interest rate in the second currency

         T is the tenor of the transaction in years.

If the second currency is the base currency, then the formula is:

$$V = P_f\, FX(1+R_f)^{-T} + P_d(1+R_d)^{-T}$$

Table 3.3 Valuation of DEM/GBP transaction

	DEM	GBP	Total
Principal amount	2,523,585	–1,000,000	
Interest rate	7%	6%	
Time to settlement	1 year	1 year	
Present value in currency	2,358,490	–943,396	
Foreign exchange rate	2.5	1.0	
Present value in GBP	943,396	–943,396	0

where the subscript f refers to the foreign currency and the subscript d refers to the domestic currency.

It can be seen that the two principal amounts are terms and conditions of the contract, as is the date on which the exchange is to take place. However, there are now three market factors of exposure which can affect the value of the transaction, namely the spot foreign exchange rate (FX), the foreign currency interest rate (R_f) and the domestic currency interest rate (R_d). Thus this transaction has three separate factor sensitivities to be calculated.

3.4.2 Example of Forward Foreign Exchange

Let us illustrate this with an example. Assume that a British institution is buying Deutschmarks against pounds sterling one year forward, and that the one-year interest rates in the two currencies are 7% and 6% respectively. The value of this contract can be calculated, using the above formula, as shown in Table 3.3

The total value of this transaction is zero, because the valuations are all done at mid-market levels and the correct forward rate is indeed 2.523585.

Table 3.4 Foreign exchange factor sensitivity

	DEM	GBP	Total
Principal amount	2,523,585	–1,000,000	
Interest rate	7%	6%	
Time to settlement	1 year	1 year	
Present value in currency	2,358,490	–943,396	
Foreign exchange rate	2.475248	1.0	
Present value in GBP	952,830	–943,396	–9,434

Table 3.5 DEM interest rate factor sensitivity

	DEM	GBP	Total
Principal amount	2,523,585	−1,000,000	
Interest rate	7.01 %	6 %	
Time to settlement	1 year	1 year	
Present value in currency	2,358,270	−943,396	
Foreign exchange rate	2.5	1.0	
Present value in GBP	943,308	−943,396	−88

The first factor sensitivity to be calculated is the sensitivity to a 1% appreciation of the Deutschmark against the pound sterling. As shown earlier, this means that the exchange rate should be changed from 2.5 to 2.5/1.01 = 2.475248. Making this substitution in the table, we obtain the new valuation shown in Table 3.4.

Thus the factor sensitivity to the DEM/GBP foreign exchange rate is negative (9,434). Note that this is not simply 1% of the principal amount of GBP 1,000,000, as was the case for a spot foreign exchange transaction. However, it is indeed 1% of the present value of the future cash flow in the base currency. Unfortunately, the present value of the future cash flow is not a number that is immediately obvious to the foreign exchange trader, so the future value is often used as a proxy. This is fine as a rough and ready estimate, but if the proxy were to be used instead of the correct calculation, this would lead to quite significant open positions, thereby exposing the institution to significant market risk.

The second factor sensitivity to be calculated is the factor sensitivity to changes in the Deutschmark interest rate. This is shown in Table 3.5, where the factor sensitivity to the Deutschmark interest rate is negative (88).

Table 3.6 GBP interest rate factor sensitivity

	DEM	GBP	Total
Principal amount	2,523,585	−1,000,000	
Interest rate	7 %	6.01 %	
Time to settlement	1 year	1 year	
Present value in currency	2,358,490	−943,307	
Foreign exchange rate	2.5	1.0	
Present value in GBP	943,396	−943,307	89

Table 3.7 Factor sensitivieties of DEM/GBP transaction

Factor sensitivities	Example 1
To 1% increase in DEM/GBP	−9,434
To 1 basis point increase in DEM rates	−88
To 1 basis point increase in GBP rates	+89

The third factor sensitivity to be calculated is the factor sensitivity to changes in the pound sterling interest rate. This is shown in Table 3.6, where the factor sensitivity to changes in the pound sterling interest rates is positive 89.

To summarize, the factor sensitivities of this forward foreign exchange transaction are as given in Table 3.7.

Note that these factor sensitivities cannot be added to obtain some form of 'total factor sensitivity' for the transaction, as they relate to different market factors. The conditions under which factor sensitivities can be added will be discussed in a later section.

3.4.3 Further Examples of Forward Foreign Exchange

Let us examine two further forward foreign exchange examples. Table 3.8 shows the foreign exchange rates and interest rates used in these examples, labelled Example 2 and Example 3.

Table 3.8 Market factor data

Currency	Spot FX	6-month rate	9-month rate	12-month rate
GBP	1.0	5%		6%
DEM	2.5		6%	7%
USD	1.5	4%	6%	

Table 3.9 Valuation of USD/GBP transaction

	USD	GBP	Total
Principal amount	−1,492,683	1,000,000	
Interest rate	4 %	5 %	
Time to settlement	6 months	6 months	
Present value in currency	−1,463,415	975,610	
Foreign exchange rate	1.5	1.0	
Present value in GBP	−975,610	975,610	0

Table 3.10 Factor sensitivities of USD/GBP transaction

Factor sensitivities	Example 2
To 1% increase in USD/GBP	–9,756
To 1 basis point increase in USD rates	+48
To 1 basis point increase in GBP rates	–48

Exaple 2 is the forward sale of USD 1,492,683 in exchange for GBP 1,000,000 for delivery in six months time. Using the same analysis as before, the present value of this contract is indeed zero, as shown in Table 3.9.

Using the same analysis as before, the factor sensitivities of this contract can be derived, and the results are given in Table 3.10.

Example 3 is selling Deutschmarks forward against US dollars. This is a forward sale of DEM 2,500,000 in exchange for USD 1,500,000 for delivery in nine months time. Using the same analysis as before, the present value of this contract is also zero, as shown in Table 3.11

The factor sensitivities of this contract can now be derived. However, in this case neither currency is the base currency of the institution, and so there are two factor sensitivities to foreign exchange rates to be calculated – the first assuming that the DEM appreciates, and the second assuming that the USD appreciates. Following the discussion earlier concerning how appreciation is to be calculated, these two factor sensitivities must be equal and opposite. The results are given in Table 3.12.

Table 3.11 Valuation of DEM/USD transaction

	DEM	USD	Total
Principal amount	–2,500,000	1,500,000	
Interest rate	6 %	6 %	
Time to settlement	9 months	9 months	
Present value in currency	–2,392,344	1,435,407	
Foreign exchange rate	2.5	1.5	
Present value in GBP	–956,938	956,938	0

Table 3.12 Factor sensitivities of DEM/USD transaction

Factor sensitivities	Example 3
To 1% increase in DEM/GBP	−9,569
To 1% increase in USD/GBP	+9,569
To 1 basis point increase in DEM rates	+69
To 1 basis point increase in USD rates	−69

3.4.4 Mathematical Derivation

The value of a forward foreign exchange transaction is given by:

$$V = P_1 FX_1 (1 + R_1)^{-T} + P_2 FX_2 (1 + R_2)^{-T}$$

where P_1 is the amount in the first foreign currency

FX_1 is the spot foreign exchange rate of currency 1

R_1 is the annual interest rate in the first currency

P_2 is the amount in the second foreign currency

FX_2 is the spot foreign exchange rate of currency 2

R_2 is the annual interest rate in the second currency

T is the tenor of the transaction in years.

This valuation formula can be differentiated with respect to each of the four underlying market factors. There are four market factors in this case, because the general formulation caters for the possibility that neither of the two foreign currencies is the base currency of the institution.

The results of these differentiations are:

$$dV / dFX_1 = P_1 (1 + R_1)^{-T}$$
$$dV / dFX_2 = P_2 (1 + R_2)^{-T}$$
$$dV / dR_1 = -TP_1 FX_1 (1 + R_1)^{-T-1}$$
$$dV / dR_2 = -TP_2 FX_2 (1 + R_2)^{-T-1}$$

These expressions for the partial derivatives of the value of the instrument are the factor sensitivities to each of the four market factors. However, as these expressions are for a unit change, they have first to be scaled down to represent a 1% change and a 0.01% change respectively.

The differentials with respect to the foreign exchange can be interpreted as the present value of the future foreign cash flow converted to the base currency of the institution at the current spot foreign exchange rate. This is similar to that for a spot foreign exchange transaction, except that the present value and the future value are identical in a spot transaction.

3.5 Equity Instruments

Factor sensitivity analysis can also be extended into the realm of equity trading, stock borrowing and equity derivatives. At its most simplistic, equity trading is identical to trading foreign currencies, with the foreign exchange rate being replaced by the stock price, and the foreign currency interest rate being replaced by the dividend yield of the equity. As there are a very large number of equities that can be traded, this approach soon leads to a very large number of market factors of exposure; the factors of exposure are no longer market factors but individual stock exposures. As a result, the approach can become rather unwieldy.

However, for those institutions where equity trading is mainly confined to trading in equity indices, the approach remains a valid one. If a small number of individual equities are also traded, a reasonable approximation is to treat these positions as positions in the index itself. A better alternative is to use the Beta coefficient of each individual stock to transform its factor sensitivity into two components, one of which has perfect correlation with the equity index and the other has zero correlation.

For trading in the equity indices, which contain many individual stocks, the treatment of the dividend yield as the equivalent of the interest rate in a foreign currency becomes a reasonable assumption, whereas with individual equities, the discrete nature of dividend payments makes this a poor assumption.

In all respects, the calculation of factor sensitivities for equity indices is similar to that for foreign exchange contracts described above.

3.6 Additivity of Factor Sensitivities

Considering the first example of a forward DEM/GBP foreign exchange contract in Section 3.4, we have three market factors and three factor sensitivities. These factor sensitivities cannot be added, as they relate to different market factors of exposure. One cannot add GBP (9,434) per 1% change in the DEM/GBP FX rate to GBP (89) per 1 basis point increase in the DEM interest rates to GBP 88 per 1 basis point increase in GBP interest rates. However, factor sensitivities to the same market factor can be added.

The factor sensitivities of the three examples can be tabulated as in Table 3.13.

The factor sensitivities to an increase in the spot value of the Deutschmark in Examples 1 and 3 can be simply added, to obtain the net sensitivity of negative 135. Because these are both sensitivities to changes in the spot rate, the tenor given against each transaction is not relevant – it does not affect the additivity of the numbers. Similarly, the factor sensitivities to an increase in the spot value of the US dollar in Examples 2 and 3 can be simply added, to obtain the net sensitivity of negative 187. The numbers in the column entitled GBP are somewhat difficult to explain, as they represent the factor sensitivity of the transaction to an increase in the value of the GBP against the GBP – clearly an impossible scenario. However, the total of positive 322 does have

Table 3.13 Sensitivity to spot FX rates

Example	Tenor (months)	Spot FX rate		
		GBP	DEM	USD
Example 2	6	9,756		(9,756)
Example 3	9		(9,569)	9,569
Example 1	12	(9,434)	9,434	
Total		322	(135)	(187)

Table 3.14 Sensitivity to interest rates

Example	Tenor (months)	Interest rates		
		GBP	DEM	USD
Example 2	6	(48)		48
Example 3	9		69	(69)
Example 1	12	89	(88)	
Total		41	(19)	(21)

some meaning – it is the change in the value of the entire portfolio for an increase in the value of the GBP against all other currencies, which is a useful figure to have available.

A similar analysis can be done for interest rates, and this is shown in Table 3.14.

The factor sensitivities to changes in interest rates in the three examples have simply been added in table 3.14. This shows that the interest rate sensitivity in one forward foreign exchange contract can be partially offset by the interest rate sensitivity in another forward foreign exchange contract. In this case, the tenor of each transaction is relevant, because interest rates at different tenors can change by different amounts, so the factor sensitivities at different tenors do not offset each other completely. The fact that this is not the case will be discussed in considerable detail in subsequent chapters.

In a large forward foreign exchange warehouse, these factor sensitivities can be very large numbers indeed. Thus they represent a significant risk that has to be carefully managed in addition to the risk of changes in foreign exchange rates.

Another extremely important use of the additivity of factor

Table 3.15 Sensitivity to interest rates

Instrument	Tenor	Factor Sensitivity
UK gilt	12	(93)
FX contract	12	89
Total		(4)

sensitivities is the ability to aggregate factor sensitivities across different lines of business. For example, if the institution held one million pounds of 8% one-year gilts in addition to the above one-year forward DEM/GBP foreign exchange transaction, the factor sensitivities would be as shown in Table 3.15

The factor sensitivity of the 1,000,000 of 8% one-year gilts to changes in GBP interest rates is negative (93). The factor sensitivity of the one-year forward DEM/GBP foreign exchange transaction to changes in GBP interest rates is positive 89. Therefore, if the institution held both positions, its total exposure to GBP interest rates would be (4).

In doing this, similar risks from completely different lines of business have been aggregated, and it is clear that the GBP interest rate risk in the foreign exchange transaction is largely offset by the GBP interest rate risk from the holding of gilts. It is this ability to aggregate factor sensitivities across different products that makes factor sensitivity analysis such a powerful tool in the management of market risk.

3.7 Comparison with Approximate Measures of Risk

Historically, there have been a great variety of measures of risk. The earliest measures were exceedingly rough and ready, but these have improved with time, due to the requirement to measure the risks inherent in huge portfolios of transactions extremely accurately.

This is best evaluated by considering the various measures that have been applied to estimate the interest rate risk of bonds with the same present values but with differing patterns of future cash flows. The true measure of interest rate risk is the change in the value of the bond for a given change in the level of interest rates.

(a) Maturity
As a first approximation, a bond with a longer maturity has a greater sensitivity to changes in interest rates than a bond with a shorter maturity, if all else is equal. This simple method assumes that interest is to be paid on the principal for the life of the bond,

and that an increase in interest rates will increase the amount of interest to be paid.

Thus, the sensitivity of a bond with principal P and maturity T in years to a one basis point change in interest rates can be approximated by the formula:

$$\Delta V = 0.01\% * P * T$$

This measure of sensitivity assumes that the sensitivity increases linearly with time, but, as was shown earlier, factor sensitivity does not increase linearly with the maturity of the instrument, but increases at a steadily decreasing rate. Clearly this a better approximation when only very short term bonds are involved, or when it is applied to very short term instruments, such as short term financial futures and forward rate agreements.

In addition, the assumption that a bond with a longer maturity is more sensitive to changes in interest rates than a bond with a shorter maturity is not necessarily true. If the longer maturity bond is an amortizing bond, this can easily be an incorrect assumption. Differences in coupon rates, payment frequencies and amortization schedules will all tend to negate the usefulness of this measure.

(b) Average Life

To overcome the problem of the amortizing bond, the average life of the bond can be calculated. This is obtained by weighting the time to each principal amortization by the amount of each principal amortization, summing the resultant weighted times and then dividing the sum by the initial principal.

Mathematically, the average life is defined as:

$$AL = \frac{\sum TiAi}{\sum Ai}$$

where AL is the average life of the bond
           Ai is the amount of the i-th amortization
           Ti is the time to the i-th amortization
and the summation is over the number of amortizations of the bond.

The sensitivity of a bond with principal P and average life AL to a one basis point change in interest rates is approximated by the formula:

$$\Delta V = 0.01\% * P * AL$$

This is certainly an improvement on using the final maturity of the bond, but it does not take interest payments into account. Because of that, the use of this sensitivity measure will mean that all bonds with the same average life are assumed to have the same sensitivity to changes in interest rates, whereas in fact a bond with a high fixed coupon has a higher sensitivity to a given change in interest rates than a similar bond with a low fixed coupon with the same average life.

There are a number of ways that this deficiency can be overcome.

(c) Modified Average Life

The first method to take account of the effect of interest payments is to use the cash flows of the bond instead of the principal amortizations. The time to each cash flow is weighted by the amount of that cash flow and included in the summation. The resultant sum is then divided by the sum of all the cash flows.

Mathematically, the modified average life is defined as:

$$MAL = \frac{\sum T_i CF_i}{\sum CF_i}$$

where MAL is the modified average life of the bond
          CF_i is the amount of the i-th cash flow
          T_i is the time to the i-th cash flow.

The sensitivity of a bond with principal P and modified average life MAL to a one basis point change in interest rates is approximated by the formula:

$$\Delta V = 0.01\% * P * MAL$$

This is an improvement on using the average life of the bond, but it ignores the fact that the absolute level of interest rates has an effect on the present value of each of these cash flows, and it is the change in the present value of the bonds that is the true determinant of interest rate risk.

(d) Effective Life

The simplest way to include the present value effect is to weight the time to each amortization by the present value rather than the future value of the amortization. This is done by multiplying the time to each principal amortization by the amount of each amortization and by the discount factor for that time, summing the resultant weighted amounts and then dividing by the sum of the amortizations weighted by the discount factors. Of course, the result of multiplying an amortization by the discount factor for that time is simply to present value the amortization.

Mathematically, the effective life is defined as:

$$EL = \frac{\sum TiAiVi}{\sum AiVi}$$

where EL is the effective life of the bond
         Ai is the amount of the i-th amortization
         Ti is the time to the i-th amortization
         Vi is the discount factor for time Ti.

The sensitivity of a bond with principal P and effective life EL to a one basis point change in interest rates is approximated by the formula:

$$\Delta V = 0.01\% * P * EL$$

This is certainly an improvement on using the average life, but it still does not take into account interest payments. Thus we need to incorporate all the cash flows of the bond and this is done in the measure known as duration.

(e) Duration

In the calculation of duration, the time to each cash flow is weighted by the present value of each cash flow before being included in the summation. The resultant sum is then divided by the sum of the present value of each of the cash flows.

Mathematically, the duration is defined as:

$$D = \frac{\sum T_i CF_i V_i}{\sum CF_i V_i}$$

where D is the duration of the bond
        CF_i is the amount of the i-th cash flow
        T_i is the time to the i-th cash flow
        V_i is the discount factor for time T_i.

Given that $V_i = (1+R)^{-T_i}$

this can be written as:

$$D = \frac{\sum T_i CF_i (1+R)^{-T_i}}{\sum CF_i (1+R)^{-T_i}}$$

This method gives a very good approximation to the sensitivity of the bond to changes in interest rates. However, the units of the above calculation are in years, not in dollars. Essentially, a bond with duration D years has the same sensitivity to a change in interest rates as a zero coupon bond of life D years.

The sensitivity of a bond with principal P and duration D to a one basis point change in interest rates is then approximated by the formula:

$$\Delta V - 0.01\% * P * D$$

However, there is still one more improvement that can be made.

(f) Modified Duration
The modified duration of a bond is the proportional change in the value of a bond for a change in interest rates. It is calculated in exactly the same manner as the duration, except that the result is divided by one plus the interest rate per period. In other words, the modified duration can be calculated using the formula:

$$MD = D \ / \ (1+R)$$

where MD is the modified duration of the bond

          D is the duration of the bond

          R is the interest rate per period.

In order to see that the definition of modified duration leads to the above simple formula, we need to use calculus, as was done in Section 3.3.3, where the factor sensitivity of a cash flow was derived mathematically by differentiating the value of the instrument with respect to its underlying market factors of exposure.

Using calculus, the definition of modified duration can be expressed as:

$$MD = (dV/dR) \ / \ V$$

Let us examine the present value of a stream of cash flows (CFi) at future times Ti. This is given by the following formula:

$$V = \sum CFi(1+R)^{-Ti}$$

where V is the present value of the bond

          CFi is the amount of the i - th cash flow

          Ti is the time to the i - th cash flow

          R is the market interest rate.

The change in this present value for a given change in the market rate can be obtained by differentiating V with respect to the rate R.

$$dV \ / \ dR = \sum(-Ti)CFi(1+R)^{-Ti-1}$$

$$= \sum(-Ti)CFi(1+R)^{-Ti} \ / \ (1+R)$$

$$= \{1/(1+R)\}\sum(-Ti)CFi(1+R)^{-Ti}$$

From the definition of duration in the previous sub-section, we have:

$$D = \sum(-Ti)CFi \ (1+R)^{-Ti} \ / \ \sum CFi(1+R)^{-Ti}$$

$$= \sum(-Ti)CFi \ (1+R)^{-Ti} \ / \ V$$

Substituting this into the expression for dV/dR, we have:

$$dV / dR = \{1 / (1 + R)\} DV$$

$$\text{or} \qquad MD = (dV / dR) / V = D / (1 + R)$$

Thus the concepts behind the modified duration of a single cash flow are identical to those behind the factor sensitivity of that cash flow. The modified duration is expressed in years and not in currency units per change in interest rates. Essentially, the modified duration of a bond is the life of the equivalent zero coupon bond, or single cash flow, that has the same sensitivity to changes in interest rates as the coupon paying bond. If a 10-year bond has a modified duration of seven years, then it will react to a parallel shift in interest rates similarly to a single cash flow at seven years that is equal in amount to the sum of all the cash flows in the 10-year bond.

The sensitivity of a bond with principal P and modified duration MD to a one basis point change in interest rates is then approximated by the formula:

$$\Delta V = 0.01\% * P * MD$$

Although the concepts behind factor sensitivity and modified duration are identical, there is no simple way of extending the terminology of modified duration to handle market factors other than interest rates. It is this major shortcoming that led to the development of the factor sensitivity approach to measuring market risk.

CHAPTER FOUR

Complex Valuation Models

4.1 Zero Coupon Interest Rate Models

4.1.1 Zero Coupon Discount Factors

The factor sensitivity analysis in the previous chapter calculated the change in the value of a position for a one basis point increase in the level of interest rates on the implicit assumption that there was only one single interest rate applicable to a given instrument. However, interest rates cannot be represented by a single number, because the interest rate is different for instruments of different tenors.

To simplify the problem, it is standard practice to take a limited range of tenor points and then quote the market yield at each of these points, thereby defining the yield curve. A typical set of tenor points, expressed in months, would be 1, 2, 3, 6, 12, 24, 36, 48, 60, 84, 120, 240 and 360 months, although sometimes additional points are added to obtain a finer grid in the early part of the yield curve, particularly at 9 months and 18 months. The market yield quoted at each tenor point is the **yield-to-maturity** and so represents the interest rate payable for an instrument of the given maturity, given that such interest is payable on a regular basis throughout the life of the instrument.

To calculate the present value of a single cash flow, a discount factor is required. However, this cannot be obtained either directly from the yield or by simple interpolation of the yields-to-maturity. This is best illustrated by looking at some simple examples.

Assume the following yield curve, in a currency in which all interest payments are made and quoted on an annual bond basis:

Table 4.1 Yield curve

Month	Rate (%)
12	7.0
24	7.5
36	8.0
48	8.5
60	9.0

If we have a one-year instrument with a principal value of 100, then there will be a single payment of 107 at the end of the first year. If this cash flow of 107 is discounted at 7%, then the par value of 100 is obtained.

Table 4.2 Present value of single cashflow

Month	Cash flow	Rate	Discount factor	Present value
12	107	7.000%	0.934579	100.000

The formula used for the discount factor is simply
$$D_n = 1 \: / \: (1 + R_n)^N ,$$
with $N = 1$ in this case.

If we have a two-year instrument with a principal value of 100, then there will be two cash flows – a payment of 7.5 at the end of the first year and a payment of 107.5 at the end of the second year. If we discount both of these payments at 7.5%, then the par value of 100 is obtained.

Table 4.3 Present value using single yield-to-maturity

Month	Cash flow	Rate	Discount factor	Present value
12	7.5	7.500%	0.930233	6.977
24	107.5	7.500%	0.865333	93.023
Total				100.000

In these two examples, the cash flows at one year (107 and 7.5 respectively) have been discounted at different rates. This implies that if the amount and the timing of a cash flow are known, then this is still insufficient information to ascertain the present value of that cash flow for a given set of market rates. This seems illogical. Why should it matter whether a given cash flow is part of a one-year instrument or a two-year instrument, when the present value of the cash flow is required? After all, a cash flow is a cash flow, and identical cash flows should be evaluated in the same manner. Clearly it would be far more sensible to discount simultaneous cash flows using identical rates. This desirable state can be achieved by treating the two-year instrument as follows.

If the one-year cash flow of 7.5 were to be discounted using the one-year rate of 7%, and the two-year cash flow of 107.5 were to be discounted at 7.5%, the resultant present value would not be the par value of 100.

Table 4.4 Present value using different yields-to-maturity

Month	Cash flow	Rate	Discount factor	Present value
12	7.5	7.000%	0.934579	7.009
24	107.5	7.500%	0.865333	93.023
Total				100.023

In order to obtain the par value of 100, having discounted the one-year cash flow using the one-year interest rate, the two-year cash flow of 107.5 must be discounted at a higher rate, namely 7.519%:

Table 4.5 Present value using zero coupon rates

Month	Cash flow	Rate	Discount factor	Present value
12	7.5	7.000%	0.934579	7.009
24	107.5	7.519%	0.865029	92.991
Total				100.000

This higher rate is known as the **zero coupon rate.** It is the rate at which to discount a single cash flow at a given point in time, regardless of whether or not there are any preceding interest payments. The discount factor derived from that rate is known as the **zero coupon discount factor**. Mathematically, these zero coupon discount factors can be derived as follows.

Consider a one-year instrument with a principal of 1, paying a coupon of Y_1 at maturity; the coupon Y_1 is the one-year yield-to-maturity rate. The final cash flow is $(1+Y_1)$, which can be discounted back to today using a discount factor D_1.

Clearly $\qquad\qquad\qquad\qquad 1 = D_1 (1+Y_1)$

Rewriting, we have: $\qquad\quad D_1 = 1 / (1 + Y_1)$

The two-year zero coupon rate is calculated by discounting the relevant series of cash flows for a two-year instrument with a principal of 1. These are Y_2, the two-year yield, paid after one year, and $(1+Y_2)$ paid after two years. These can be discounted back to today, using the appropriate discount factors D_1 and D_2. This must result in the par value of 1.

$$1 = D_1 Y_2 + D_2 (1+Y_2)$$

Rewriting, we have: $D_2 = (1 - Y_2 D_1) / (1 + Y_2)$

Similarly, the three-year discount factor can be calculated to be:

$$D_3 = (1 - Y_3 D_1 - Y_3 D_2) / (1+Y_3)$$

The general formula for the zero coupon rate can be derived by setting out the cash flows for each year, and then calculating their present value, in the same manner as above:

$$\begin{aligned}
\text{Principal} &= 1 \\
\text{Tenor} &= N \\
\text{Yield} &= Y_n \\
\text{Discount factor} &= D_n
\end{aligned}$$

$$\text{Present value} = 1 = Y_n D_1 + Y_n D_2 + \ldots + (1+Y_n)D_n$$

Thus $\qquad\qquad D_N = \left(1 - Y_n \sum D_i\right) / \left(1+Y_n\right)$

where the sum is over all values of i less than N.

This gives the discount factor D_n in terms of the discount factors for shorter tenors. Given that $D_1 = 1 / (1+Y_1)$, then the above formula can be applied successively to obtain the zero coupon discount factors (ZCDF) for all years up to and including D_n. The zero coupon discount factor can then be converted back to a zero coupon rate (ZCR), by using the formula:

$$D_n = 1 / (1 + R_n)^N$$

The results for the sample yield curve above are shown in Table 4.6.

Table 4.6 Zero coupon rates

Month	Rate (%)	ZCDF	ZCR
12	7.0	0.934579	7.000
24	7.5	0.865029	7.519
36	8.0	0.792622	8.055
48	8.5	0.718581	8.613
60	9.0	0.644061	9.198

This does require that the yield is known for every year to maturity, which is not normally a problem up to five years. For the longer tenors that are not normally quoted, such as 6, 8 and 9 years, the yield-to-maturity is normally derived by simple linear interpolation between the 5, 7 and 10-year rates.

This is essentially a bootstrap method, because in order to calculate the zero coupon discount factor at a given tenor, all the discount factors for shorter tenors are required. Because all the relationships are linear, these can be specified as a set of simultaneous linear equations, and so an alternative formulation using a matrix inversion procedure could be specified.

The above derivation of zero coupon discount factors is equally valid using continuously compounding rates. It would appear that the discount factor for one year should be given by $D_1 = e^{-R_1}$ instead of by $D_1 = 1 / (1+Y_1)$, but the relationship between the quoted annual rate and the continuously compounding rate is such that these two discount factors are identical. The bootstrap method involves discount factors only, and so remains perfectly valid; the zero coupon discount factors are the same. However, if the zero coupon discount factors were to be converted back to continuously compounding rates, this would have to be done using the formula $D_n = e^{-R_n N}$ rather than the formula $D_n = 1/(1+R_n)^N$, and this will give slightly different zero coupon rates as they are continuously compounding rates. Both sets of zero coupon rates are shown in Table 4.7.

For currencies in which the yields are quoted on a semi-annual basis, the general formula has to be modified to work on a semi-annual basis.

Table 4.7 Zero coupon rates

Month	Rate (%)	ZCDF	ZCR (Annual)	ZCR (Continuous)
12	7.0	0.934579	7.000	6.766
24	7.5	0.865029	7.519	7.250
36	8.0	0.792622	8.055	7.747
48	8.5	0.718581	8.613	8.262
60	9.0	0.644061	9.198	8.799

$$D_n = \left(1 - \tfrac{1}{2}Y_n \sum_{i=\frac{1}{2}}^{n-\frac{1}{2}} D_i\right) / \left(1 + \tfrac{1}{2}Y_n\right)$$

This formula calculates the semi-annual discount factors. This is necessary for the semi-annual currencies, such as US dollars and pounds sterling and Japanese yen. Most European currencies are quoted annually. To use this formula, the semi-annual rate is required at each semi-annual point on the maturity grid. As rates are not usually quoted for half years, the half-yearly yield-to-maturity rates are obtained by interpolating between the quoted yearly yield-to-maturity rates.

In the above derivation, there is an implicit assumption that each coupon payment is equal to the yield Y_n, or $\tfrac{1}{2}Y_n$, for a principal of one. However, where the rate is quoted on an actual over 360 or actual over 365 basis, the exact number of days in each interest period should be used to obtain the fractional period, rather than assuming it is either 1 or $\tfrac{1}{2}$. Although this makes the formula look somewhat complicated, the essential logic is unchanged.

Another problem that can arise in practice is that there is a point on the maturity grid for which no reliable market rates exist. In particular, this can happen in minor currencies where the maturity grid is set to be the same as for the major currencies. The usual solution to this problem is to interpolate the yield at the required point from the two adjacent points on the grid at which market rates are known.

For unusual tenors, it is essential to know how the basis on which the yield is quoted. For example, the 18-month market rate is quoted on three different bases, depending on the currency.

There could be three semi-annual interest payments; there could be two payments, the first at 6 months and the second at 18 months; or there could be two payments, the first at 12 months and the second at 18 months. The correct payment schedule must be used when calculating the zero coupon discount factor at 18 months.

By using these zero coupon discount factors, any stream of arbitrary cash flows can be valued. This is particularly important when valuing complex interest rate swaps with irregular amortization schedules. However, the above method only gives the zero coupon discount factors at the known points on the maturity grid. To value a cash flow that is not at a point on the maturity grid, some form of interpolation is required. The various interpolation techniques are described in Section 4.2.

4.1.2 Forward Rates

In order to value certain instruments, such as forward rate agreements, it is necessary to calculate the forward rate. This is the rate, for example, that should be applied to the period of one year starting one year from today, or to the period of two years starting one year from today. These forward rates are calculated using zero coupon discount factors.

Table 4.8 Annual zero coupon rates

Month	Rate (%)	ZCDF	ZCR (Annual)
12	7.0	0.934579	7.000
24	7.5	0.865029	7.519
36	8.0	0.792622	8.055

In the previous section, zero coupon discount factors and zero coupon rates were calculated for a sample yield curve.

The zero coupon rate is calculated from the zero coupon discount factor using the formula:

$$D_n = 1 / (1 + R_n)^N$$

Based on these zero coupon discount factors, an investment of 1 will have a future value of $(1/0.934579) = 1.07$ after one year. Similarly an investment of 1 will have a future value of $(1/0.865029) = 1.156031$ after two years. This means that an investment of 1.07 made in one year's time will grow to 1.156031 after a further year. By scaling these figures down, we see that an investment of 1 made in one year's time will grow to $(1.156031/1.07) = 1.080402$ after a further year. This can be calculated even more directly from the ratio of the zero coupon discount factors, since $(0.934579/0.865029) = 1.080402$. Thus, the one- to two-year forward rate is 8.040 % as an annual rate.

Similarly, the one- to three-year forward rate can be calculated. A sum of $(1/0.934579)$ in one year's time will grow to $(1/0.792622)$ in three years' time. Thus the growth over the two-year period starting in one year's time is $(0.934579/0.792622) = 1.179098$. As this represents the compounded growth over the two years, we must now use the formula:

$$FV = PV(1+R)^T \quad \text{where} \quad T = 2$$
$$FV / PV = (1+R)^2 = 1.179098$$
$$(1+R) = 1.085863$$
$$R = 8.586\%$$

The one- to three-year forward rate is therefore 8.586 %.

Exactly the same methodology can be applied using continuously compounded rates. The zero coupon discount factors and the continuously compounding zero coupon rates were calculated for a sample yield curve.

Table 4.9 Continuous zero coupon rates

Month	Rate (%)	ZCDF	ZCR (Continuous)
12	7.0	0.934579	6.766
24	7.5	0.865029	7.250
36	8.0	0.792622	7.747

The zero coupon rate is calculated from the zero coupon discount factor using the formula:

$$D_n = e^{-R_n N}$$

As before, an investment of 1 will have a future value of $(1/0.934579) = 1.07$ after one year. Similarly an investment of 1 will have a future value of $(1/0.865029) = 1.156031$ after two years. This means that an investment of 1.07 made in one year's time will grow to 1.156031 after a further year. By scaling these figures down, we see that an investment of 1 made in one year's time will grow to $(1.156031/1.07) = 1.080402$ after a further year. This can be calculated even more directly from the ratio of the zero coupon discount factors, since $(0.934579/0.865029) = 1.080402$. When this is converted to a continuously compounding rate, the one- to two-year forward rate is 7.733 % continuously compounding.

Similarly, the one- to three-year forward rate can be calculated. A sum of $(1/0.934579)$ in one year's time will grow to $(1/0.792622)$ in three years' time. Thus the growth over the two-year period starting in one year's time is $(0.934579/0.792622) = 1.179098$. As this represents the compounded growth over the two years, we must now use the formula:

$$FV = PV\, e^{RT} \qquad \text{where } T = 2$$
$$FV / PV = e^{RT} = 1.179098$$
$$RT = \ln(1.179098) = 0.164750$$
$$R = 8.237\%$$

The one- to three-year forward rate is therefore 8.237 % continuously compounding.

4.2 Interpolation Techniques

There are many methods that have been used to interpolate between two points on a maturity grid, but quite a few of these are inappropriate for the valuation of arbitrary cash flows. These include the many methods of interpolating between known yields-to-maturity, and as we have seen, yield-to-maturity is not a particularly useful concept for valuation purposes, except insofar as it provides the source of market input data to the calculation of zero coupon discount factors.

There are two techniques that have gained widespread acceptance. These are the exponential interpolation of zero coupon discount factors and the linear interpolation of zero coupon rates. The exponential interpolation of zero coupon discount factors can also be derived from the assumption of a constant continuously compounding forward rate.

4.2.1 Exponential Interpolation of Zero Coupon Discount Factors

Let us calculate the discount factor D at time T, which lies between two known points on the maturity grid T_1 and T_2. The zero coupon discount factor at time T_1 is D_1 and the zero coupon discount factor at time T_2 is D_2.

From the definition of a zero coupon discount factor, we can see that if a unit of currency is invested at time $T=0$, then it will have grown to $(1/D_1)$ at time T_1 and to $(1/D_2)$ by time T_2. Using continuous compounding interest rates, we have:

$$(1/D_1) = \exp(R_1 T_1)$$

and $$(1/D_2) = \exp(R_2 T_2)$$

If we define R_f to be the forward continuous compounding interest rate from time T_1 to time T_2, then we have:

$$(1/D_2) = (1/D_1) \exp(R_f (T_2 - T_1))$$

or $$(D_1/D_2) = \exp(R_f (T_2 - T_1))$$

Taking the natural logarithm of both sides:

$$\ln(D_1/D_2) = R_f (T_2 - T_1)$$

or $$R_f = \{1 / (T_2 - T_1)\} \ln (D_1/D_2)$$

The rate of growth implied by this forward rate can also be assumed to apply to the partial period from time T_1 to time T. This implies:

$$(1/D) = (1/ D_1) \exp(R_f (T - T_1))$$

Substituting for R_f from above, we have

$$(D_1/D) = \exp [\{(T-T_1)/ (T_2-T_1)\} \ln (D_1/D_2)]$$

To simplify the expression, define f as the ratio of $(T-T_1)$ to (T_2-T_1). In symbols:

$$f = (T-T_1)/ (T_2-T_1)$$

Thus we have

$$(D_1/D) = \exp [f \ln (D_1/D_2)]$$
$$= \exp [\ln (D_1/D_2)^f]$$
$$= (D_1/D_2)^f$$

Rearranging: $D = D_1^{(1-f)} D_2^f$

This is the formula for exponential interpolation of zero coupon discount factors.

4.2.2 Linear Interpolation of Zero Coupon Rates

The second commonly used interpolation technique is to linearly interpolate the zero coupon rates. In some cases, the effective annual zero coupon rates are used, whereas in other cases the continuously compounded zero coupon rates are used. For mathematical simplicity, we shall use the continuously compounded zero coupon rates. As will be seen later, the difference between using continuously compounded rates and annual rates is quite small.

Let us calculate the discount factor D at time T, which time lies between two known points on the maturity grid T_1 and T_2. The zero coupon discount factor at time T_1 is D_1 and the zero coupon discount factor at time T_2 is D_2.

From the definition of a zero coupon discount factor, we can see that if a unit of currency is invested at time $T-0$, then it will have grown to $(1/D_1)$ at time T_1 and to $(1/D_2)$ by time T_2. Using continuous compounding interest rates, we have:

$$(1/D_1) = \exp(R_1 T_1)$$

and $\quad (1/D_2) = \exp(R_2 T_2)$

Using the definition of the fractional period of time used above, we can linearly interpolate the zero coupon rates as follows:

$$R = R_1 + f(R_2 - R_1)$$

This can now be used to calculate the discount factor:

$$
\begin{aligned}
D &= \exp(-RT) \\
&= \exp\left\{(-R_1 - f(R_2 - R_1))T\right\} \\
&= \exp(-R_1(1-f)T)\ \exp(-R_2 fT) \\
&= \exp\left[-R_1 T_1(T/T_1)(1-f)\right]\ \exp\left[-R_2 T_2(T/T_2)f\right] \\
&= \left[\exp(-R_1 T_1)\right] \wedge \left\{(T/T_1)(1-f)\right\}\ \left[\exp(-R_2 T_2)\right] \wedge \left((T/T_2)f\right) \\
&= [D_1] \wedge \left\{(T/T_1)(1-f)\right\}\ [D_2] \wedge \left\{(T/T_2)f\right\}
\end{aligned}
$$

This formula is similar to that for exponential interpolation of zero coupon discount factors. However, it differs in the weight applied to the two discount factors. The first term has an extra (T/T_1) term multiplying the $(1-f)$ exponent, whereas the second term has an extra (T/T_2) term multiplying the (f) exponent. Note that these weightings can cause severe problems in computer programs when $T_1 = 0$, as this results in a division by zero. However, this case can be handled separately, as D_1 is then equal to 1 and so D_1 raised to any power must be 1.

4.2.3 Differences Between Interpolation Methods

The difference in valuation between these two interpolation techniques is fairly small, but is certainly not insignificant . An example will serve to illustrate the magnitude of the difference. Let us use the zero coupon discount factors for 12 months and 24 months shown in Table 4.10 that were calculated in the previous section.

If there is a cash flow of 1,000,000 at 18 months, the two valuation methods will give the different answers shown in Table 4.11, namely 899,132 and 900,220.

In the above analysis, the result for linear interpolation is based on the formula derived for continuously compounding rates. When the calculation is done using linear interpolation of the annual zero coupon rates, the resultant value becomes 900,216

Table 4.10 Interpolation of discount factors

	Month	Yield (%)	Discount factor	ZCR (Annual)
	12	7.0	0.934579	7.000
	24	7.5	0.865029	7.519
Exponential	18		0.899132	
Linear	18		0.900220	7.259

Table 4.11 Interpolation methods

Exponential interpolation	899,132
Linear interpolation	900,220
Difference	1,088

instead of 900,220. Even this small difference suggests that the linear interpolation should be done directly, if the entire revaluation procedure is based on annual rates.

The difference of 1,088 represents a percentage difference of about 0.1% or 10 basis points – a number comparable to the bid-offer spreads available in the market place. With steeper yield curves, the difference becomes even more significant.

Another important difference between the two interpolation methods concerns the assignment of factor sensitivities to the points on the maturity grid. This will be discussed further in Section 5.1.4.

4.3 Interest Rate Derivatives

An interest rate swap is an agreement to exchange a stream of fixed interest rate payments for a stream of floating interest rate payments.

To value the swap, these fixed interest payments are discounted using the zero coupon discount factors calculated as outlined earlier in this chapter. In addition, the notional principal is included as a fixed payment at the final maturity date. Then the next interest payment on the floating leg, which has already been fixed, is discounted from the next interest payment date together with the notional principal. These two present values are then netted against each other to obtain the value of the swap.

A similar method is used to value a cross-currency swap, in which the two interest payment streams are in different currencies. Two sets of zero coupon discount factors are required, one set for each currency. The spot foreign exchange rate is then used to convert from one currency to the other, before netting the two present values against each other. In both swaps, it is the set of fixed interest payments and notional principals that is required to evaluate the factor sensitivities of the transaction. This is detailed in Chapter 5.

Forward rate agreements pay the difference between an agreed rate for a period and the actual floating rate for the period, discounted from the end of the period to the beginning of the period, and paid on the settlement date at the beginning of the period. Between trade date and settlement date, the forward rate agreement is valued using the forward rate as the actual floating rate, where the forward rate is calculated from the zero coupon discount factors as shown in Section 4.1.2. It can be shown that the factor sensitivity of a forward rate agreement is the factor sensitivity of two cash flows – an inflow of the principal at the beginning of the period and an outflow of the principal and the agreed rate of interest at the end of the period. The notional principal can be either positive or negative.

4.4 Foreign Exchange Options

Although the derivation of the Black-Scholes valuation formula is considered beyond the scope of this book, the formula itself can be given and analysed.

The valuation formula is as follows:

$$V = S \; \exp\left(-R_f \, T\right) \, N(d_1) - X \exp\left(-R_d \, T\right) \, N(d_2)$$

$$d_1 = \left[\ln\left\{\left(S \exp\left(-R_f \, T\right)\right) / \left(X \exp\left(-R_d \, T\right)\right)\right\} / \left\{\sigma \sqrt{T}\right\}\right] + 0.5\,\sigma\sqrt{T}$$

$$d_2 = \left[\ln\left\{\left(S \exp\left(-R_f \, T\right)\right) / \left(X \exp\left(-R_d \, T\right)\right)\right\} / \left\{\sigma \sqrt{T}\right\}\right] - 0.5\,\sigma\sqrt{T}$$

where S is the spot foreign exchange rate

            X is the strike price of the option

            R_f is the foreign currency interest rate

            R_d is the domestic currency interest rate

            T is the time to the expiry of the option

            σ is the volatility of the foreign exchange rate

and $N(.)$ is the cumulative normal distribution function.

Despite the mathematical complexity of this formula, it can be readily analysed to see that there are now four market factors required for the valuation of this transaction, namely the spot foreign exchange rate S, the foreign currency interest rate R_f, the domestic currency interest rate R_d, and the volatility of the foreign exchange rate σ – a new market factor.

Because of this mathematical complexity – and this is the valuation formula for the simplest option – the market risk for option portfolios will not be handled with the same rigour as is the case for the simpler products. However, sufficient detail will be included to incorporate options into the same framework as all other products.

CHAPTER FIVE

Complex Factor Sensitivity Analysis

5.1 Detailed Factor Sensitivity Analysis

In the discussion on zero coupon discount factors it was noted that the yield curve is defined by a set of discrete yields at a limited number of tenor points. A typical set of tenor points, expressed in months, would be 1, 2, 3, 6, 12, 24, 36, 48, 60, 84, 120, 240 and 360 months, although sometimes additional points are added to obtain a finer grid in the early part of the yield curve. There are 13 tenor points in this list, but it has now become almost standard practice to include yields at 9 and 18 months as well, making 15 tenor points in all.

In the discussion on factor sensitivity analysis, the sensitivity to changes in interest rates was calculated on the basis that only one interest rate was required to value the instrument in question. However, with the use of zero coupon valuation techniques, all 15 points on the yield curve are input into the valuation process, so it would seem sensible to calculate a separate sensitivity to a one basis point change in each individual yield. In essence, we are redefining the factor sensitivity to interest rates as 15 separate factor sensitivities.

5.1.1 Simple Portfolio of Bonds

The method described above is used in the following portfolio of annual bonds, each of which has a tenor exactly equal to a point on the maturity grid. Each bond has a coupon equal to the yield-

Table 5.1 Factor sensitivity of bond portfolio

Maturity	Face value	Coupon (%)	Factor sensitivity
1	(100)	7.00	9,345
2	(100)	7.50	17,953
3	(100)	8.00	25,766
7	100	9.50	(49,480)
10	100	9.75	(62,084)
30	100	10.00	(94,191)
Total	0		(152,690)

to-maturity for that tenor. The face value is expressed in millions, but the factor sensitivity to changes in interest rates is given in individual currency units (see Table 5.1).

This portfolio of bonds has total face value of zero – the value of the long positions is equal to the value of the short positions. Even though the portfolio is evenly balanced in this respect, it is by no means risk free. An increase in the 30-year rate of one basis point will result in a loss of 94,191; an increase in the 1-year rate of one basis point will result in a gain of 9,345. In all, there are six such factor sensitivities in Table 5.1; one for each bond position. However, an increase in all yields of one basis point will result in a loss of 152,690 – a considerable sum for a portfolio of this size, simply because the gains do not offset the losses.

On the other hand, if the three short positions were made some four times larger, then the portfolio would be appear to be unbalanced in that the net position is now short by a total of 830 million. This apparent imbalance can be corrected by placing the difference of 830 million in the overnight money market. Such a short tenor placement will not contribute any factor sensitivity to the portfolio – by the time the interest rates can change overnight, the placement will have matured (Table 5.2).

With these larger positions, an increase in the 30-year rate of one basis point will still result in a loss of 94,191, but an increase in the 1-year rate of one basis point will now result in a gain of 30,838. The total gains now offset the total losses, so that an increase in all yields of one basis point will result in a loss of a mere 38.

Table 5.2 Factor sensitivity of bond portfolio

Maturity	Face value	Coupon (%)	Factor sensitivity
1	(330)	7.00	30,838
2	(400)	7.50	71,813
3	(400)	8.00	103,065
7	100	9.50	(49,480)
10	100	9.75	(62,084)
30	100	10.00	(94,191)
Total	(830)		(38)

The sign on the total factor sensitivity is not important in this context. Because changes in interest rates could be either upwards or downwards, it is the absolute magnitude of the factor sensitivity that is important. Clearly, a factor sensitivity of 38 is very small for a portfolio of this size, unlike the 152,690 of the previous example.

The above examples showed factor sensitivities to six different points on the maturity grid, and a full example would have shown 15 factor sensitivities. Thus it is of some importance to establish whether the six factor sensitivities shown are a complete description of the sensitivity of this portfolio to changes in interest rates, or whether the entire 15 factor sensitivities are required.

5.1.2 Factor Sensitivity to Yield-to-Maturity Rates

Whether factor sensitivities are required at every point on the maturity grid will depend upon exactly which interest rates are used in the factor sensitivity calculation. The rates that are to be increased by one basis point are the yield-to-maturity rates, and not the zero coupon rates. Some of the reasons for this choice are given later in this section.

Let us examine the factor sensitivity of a one million-pound, two-year bond with an annual coupon of 7.5%. First of all, the zero coupon discount factors are used to value the bond, and these give a value of par, as shown in Table 5.3.

Let us start by calculating the factor sensitivity to the two-year interest rate. This is found by increasing the two-year yield-to-maturity rate by one basis point, performing the valuation again

Table 5.3 Valuation of two-year bond

Month	Yield-to-maturity	Zero rate	Discount factor	Cash flow	Present value
12	7.00%	7.000%	0.934579	75,000	70,093.46
24	7.50%	7.519%	0.865029	1,075,000	929,906.54
Total					1,000,000.00

Table 5.4 Factor sensitivity to two-year rate

Month	Yield-to-maturity	Zero rate	Discount factor	Cash flow	Present value
12	7.00%	7.000%	0.934579	75,000	70,093.46
24	7.51%	7.519%	0.864862	1,075,000	929,726.60
Total					999,820.06
Difference					(179.94)

and taking the difference (Table 5.4).

Let us now calculate the factor sensitivity to the one-year interest rate. This is found by increasing the one-year yield-to-maturity rate by one basis point, performing the valuation again and taking the difference (Table 5.5).

This is an interesting result. It shows that there is no factor sensitivity to a change in the one-year rate, in spite of the fact that the bond has a cash flow at one year. The present value of that cash flow has indeed changed because the increase in the one-year yield-to-maturity rate has resulted in a change in the one-year discount factor. However, there has been no change in the value of the two-year bond, and this is entirely correct. The market rate for a two-year bond is still 7.5%, even though the one-year rate has changed. Since the two-year rate has not changed from 7.5% and the coupon rate for the two-year bond is still 7.5%, there should be no change whatsoever in the value of the two-year bond. This result is exactly what one should expect from a sensible factor sensitivity system.

The mathematics of zero coupon discounting, as shown in the

Table 5.5 Factor sensitivity to one-year rate

Month	Yield-to-maturity	Zero rate	Discount factor	Cash flow	Present value
12	7.01%	7.010%	0.934492	75,000	70,086.91
24	7.50%	7.518%	0.865035	1,075,000	929,913.09
Total					1,000,000.00
Difference					0.00

above example, ensures that there is no factor sensitivity. The increase in the one-year rate gives a decrease in the one-year zero coupon discount factor, so the present value of the interest payment at the one-year mark decreases. However, this decrease in the one-year zero coupon discount factor also results in an increase in the two-year zero coupon discount factor, such that the present value of the two-year cash flow increases. The value of this increase in the present value of the two-year cash flow exactly offsets the decrease in the present value of the one-year cash flow. Consequently, changes in the one-year rate have no effect whatsoever on the value of a two-year bond.

This interesting result only holds if the two-year bond is an on-market bond. If the coupon on the two year bond is not equal to the two-year yield-to-maturity, then the mathematics does not result in an exact compensation. There is then some factor sensitivity to the one-year interest rate, effectively arising from the amount of the interest payment which represents an off-market payment. For example, consider a coupon of 10% on the two-year bond (Tables 5.6 and 5.7).

The factor sensitivity to the one-year rate is now negative 2.03. This can be shown to be the factor sensitivity of the off-market cash flows of 25,000 at one and two years.

Returning to the factor sensitivity of an on-market two-year bond, it should be noted that the factor sensitivity of 179.94

Table 5.6 Valuation of off-market bond

Month	Yield-to-maturity	Discount factor	Cash flow	Present value
12	7.00%	0.934492	100,000	93,457.94
24	7.50%	0.865035	1,100,000	951,532.28
Total				1,044,990.22

Table 5.7 Factor sensitivity to one-year rate

Month	Yield-to-maturity	Discount factor	Cash flow	Present value
12	7.01%	0.934492	100,000	93,449.21
24	7.50%	0.865035	1,100,000	951,538.98
Total				1,044,988.19
Difference				(2.03)

shown in Table 5.4 is not an exact scaling of the factor sensitivity of 17,953 shown in Table 5.1 for a 100 million bond. It is not identical, because the earlier result was on the assumption that both cash flows were to be discounted at 7.50% and then at 7.51%, the difference being the factor sensitivity. In this case, changes in the two-year yield-to-maturity rate only affect cash flows that occur after the tenor point on the maturity grid that immediately precedes the two-year point – in this case the one-year point.

This result is a general one, not restricted to two-year bonds. Any on-market bond will only have a factor sensitivity to the yield-to-maturity of its final tenor. For example, the entire factor sensitivity of a 10-year bond with a 9.75% coupon will be to the 10-year yield-to-maturity, when the current 10-year rate is 9.75%. There will be no factor sensitivity to rates of less than 10 years.

Because the portfolio in Section 5.1.1 was comprised of on-market bonds whose tenors fell exactly on the given points on the maturity grid, the entire factor sensitivity of each bond will fall into the appropriate single point on the maturity grid, with all other factor sensitivities being zero. Thus the entire detailed factor sensitivity can be described by the six factor sensitivities, rather than needing the entire grid of 15 factor sensitivities.

However, there are some systems in use today which calculate the factor sensitivities to the zero coupon rates. These systems will give a factor sensitivity at the one-year mark for an on-market two-year bond. Such a system can certainly be used, but it does have certain limitations. One of these is that an on-market instrument will appear to change in value when some other interest rate changes. The second is that changes in market rates are seen by traders as changes in yields-to-maturity, and not as changes in zero coupon rates. A third more significant problem will be revealed when we discuss Value at Risk.

5.1.3 More Complex Portfolio of Bonds

In Section 5.1.1, the portfolio consisted of bonds whose coupons were all exactly on-market. Let us now consider a similar portfolio in which the coupons are off-market, together with a different yield curve. The factor sensitivities to the yield-to-maturity of each

Table 5.8 Factor sensitivity of complex bond portfolio

Maturity	Face	Coupon (%)	Market yield (%)	Factor sensitivity
1	100	7.50	8.00	(9,216)
2	100	8.25	7.80	(17,990)
3	100	9.00	7.60	(26,612)
7	(100)	9.50	7.50	56,604
10	(100)	9.25	7.40	74,760
30	(100)	8.75	7.30	137,523
Total	0			215,069

Table 5.9 Factor sensitivity of complex bond portfolio

Maturity	Face	Coupon (%)	Market yield (%)	Factor sensitivity
1	500	7.50	8.00	(46,078)
2	500	8.25	7.80	(89,949)
3	500	9.00	7.60	(133,060)
7	(100)	9.50	7.50	56,604
10	(100)	9.25	7.40	74,760
30	(100)	8.75	7.30	137,523
Total	1200			(200)

bond can be calculated, and the results are shown in Table 5.8.

Once again there is a very significant factor sensitivity to a one basis point increase in the yield-to-maturity. This can be eliminated by taking positions that are five times larger in the first three bonds (Table 5.9).

This has reduced the factor sensitivity to a mere 200, which is very small for a position of over one billion in face value.

Although this factor sensitivity is small, it is the change in value of the portfolio if all yields were to increase by one basis point. Since we have a portfolio of six bonds of different tenors, it is quite possible for the market yields to increase at some tenors and decrease at other tenors. The resultant change in value would be very different, if, for example, the market yields at 1, 2 and 3 years were to increase by one basis point while the market yields at 7, 10 and 30 years were to decrease. In this example, the result would be a loss of 537,974 in this portfolio with a net face value of 1,200,000,000. This is a very significant risk indeed.

Table 5.10 Factor sensitivity of individual bonds

Month	30Yr	10Yr	7Yr	3Yr	2Yr	1Yr	Total
12	16	83	111	(555)	(179)	(46,078)	(46,603)
24	33	172	231	(1,156)	(86,693)	0	(90,414)
36	51	269	361	(131,404)	0	0	(130,724)
48	71	372	499	0	0	0	943
60	149	786	1,054	0	0	0	1,990
84	372	1,958	54,240	0	0	0	56,569
120	2,047	70,814	0	0	0	0	72,861
240	7,228	0	0	0	0	0	7,228
360	126,972	0	0	0	0	0	126,972
Total	136,939	74,454	56,495	(133,115)	(89,872)	(46,078)	(1,178)

Such a risk would only be contemplated if there were strong reasons to believe that the market yields would move in the opposite direction. As the yield curve in this example is inverted, there could be a strong argument that it would move to become a flat or normal yield curve, rather than becoming even more inverted.

Using the second portfolio of bonds, the factor sensitivities of each bond can be shown to the yield-to-maturity at each point on the maturity grid. The results are given in Table 5.10.

In this table, the detailed factor sensitivities of each bond are shown in separate columns. The total factor sensitivities to the interest rates at each point in the maturity grid are then shown in the final column, which simply sums the factor sensitivities of each individual bond. The factor sensitivity of the entire portfolio of bonds to a one basis point increase in all interest rates – a parallel shift in the yield curve – is given in the bottom right hand corner of the table as (1,178).

It can be seen that the net total factor sensitivity (1,178) differs from that given earlier in Table 5.9 (200), as do the total factor sensitivities for each bond. The reason for this is that Table 5.10 shows the factor sensitivity to the interest rate at each point on the maturity grid, these factor sensitivities are then simply added together to obtain the total factor sensitivity. This does not give exactly the same result as calculating the factor sensitivity to a parallel shift of one basis point in all interest rates, because there are non-linearities in the calculation – the effect of increasing a yield by one basis point is not exactly twice the effect of increasing the same yield by half a basis point.

5.1.4 Allocation of Factor Sensitivities

In the previous section, the allocation of factor sensitivities to the various points on the maturity grid was a moderately simple task, because all the cash flows fell exactly on the points of the maturity grid. This is not true in the general case, so a method is needed to allocate factor sensitivities of cash flows to the points on the maturity grid. This is a logical extension of the valuation process using zero coupon discount factors.

The current yield-to-maturity curve is used to generate the zero-coupon discount factors at each point on the maturity grid. Each of the cash flows of the bond is then present valued, using the interpolation method explained in Section 4.2.1 – the exponential interpolation of zero coupon discount factors. These present values are then summed to obtain the total value of the portfolio. Next, just one yield-to-maturity is increased by one basis point, and the entire set of zero-coupon discount factors is calculated again and used to obtain the total present value of the portfolio. The difference between these two valuations is the factor sensitivity of the portfolio to a one basis point increase in rates at that particular point on the maturity grid. This process is then repeated for every point on the yield curve, thereby obtaining the entire total factor sensitivity vector, displayed in the right-hand column in Table 5.10. Thus the factor sensitivity of a cash flow that falls between two points on the maturity grid will be assigned automatically to the two adjacent points.

Because all the zero coupon discount factors are re-calculated for each change in yield, this process would appear to require a significant amount of processing time. However, given the speed of modern computers, even large portfolios can be processed in minutes rather than hours.

The two major interpolation techniques result in completely different allocations of the factor sensitivities of a given cash flow to the two adjacent points on the maturity grid. Again, this is best illustrated with an example. Let us examine how the factor sensitivity of a cash flow of 1,000,000 is allocated between the three-month and six-month points on the maturity grid. This is shown in Figure 5.1.

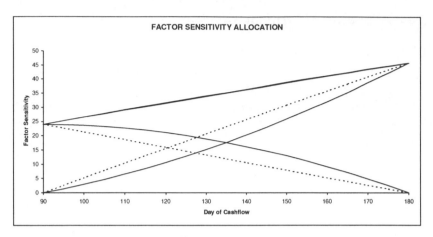

Figure 5.1   Factor sensitivity allocation

The two continuous lines which cross in the centre of the graph are based on linear interpolation of the continuous compounding zero coupon rate; these lines are smooth curves. The two dotted lines are based on exponential interpolation of the zero coupon discount factors; these lines are practically straight lines. The upper line is in fact two lines – the sum of the two allocated factor sensitivities – for the two different interpolation techniques. The two techniques give total factor sensitivities that are very similar, so much so that they cannot be distinguished from each other when plotted on this scale.

Both pairs of lines show how the factor sensitivity of the 1,000,000 cash flow is allocated between the three-month (90-day) bucket and the six-month (180-day) bucket. When the cash flow is at 90 days, the entire factor sensitivity of 24.03 is allocated to the three-month bucket. When the cash flow is at 180 days, the entire factor sensitivity of 45.78 is allocated to the six-month bucket. For times in between, the factor sensitivities at three months and six months can be read from the graph.

Of particular interest is the allocation of the total factor sensitivity at the mid-point, which is when the cash flow is at 135 days. Using the linear interpolation of zero coupon rates, the allocations to three and six months are identical. Using the exponential interpolation of zero coupon discount factors, the allocations to three and six months are in the ratio of one-third to two-thirds, which is the ratio of the factor sensitivities at three months and six months, which is more precisely 24.03 to 45.78.

5.1.5 Multiple Yield Curves

In the above discussion of detailed factor sensitivities, it was stated that the factor sensitivity of a portfolio of fixed interest rate instruments should be calculated, not to a single yield-to-maturity rate, but to each of a set of 15 yield-to-maturity rates, namely 1, 2, 3, 6, 9, 12, 18, 24, 36, 48, 60, 84, 120, 240 and 360 months.

This is, of course, on the assumption that all the instruments in the portfolio can be valued off the same yield curve. In practice, this is most unlikely. Although a book of swaps should be valued using the swap yield curve, the imbalance between the long and the short swaps will be hedged by other instruments in the portfolio, such as short term money market instruments and longer term government bonds. These will be valued using their own yield curves – the money market yield curve and the government yield curve.

Although there is a distinct money market yield curve in certain currencies at tenors beyond one year, the yield curve below one year is often treated as if it were identical to the swap yield curve. This is done by constructing the shorter end of the swap yield curve from money market instruments, such as cash rates and money market futures.

In order to calculate the factor sensitivity of an instrument, a yield curve is needed to value the instrument using the current market rate, and then using the current market rate increased by one basis point. However, as we have seen, the factor sensitivity itself is fairly insensitive to small changes in the market rates at which it is calculated. Thus if the factor sensitivities were to be calculated using a slightly inaccurate yield curve, they would still be sufficiently accurate to manage the risk in the portfolio. This is an extremely useful result, as it means that the factor sensitivities of a bond portfolio of investment-grade counterparties can be calculated using the swap yield curve as a proxy for the bond yield curve, as the two yield curves would not differ greatly from one another. In this context, the two yield curves can be tens of basis points apart without affecting the results significantly.

However, this does not apply to a portfolio of non-investment-grade bonds (often called 'junk bonds'), because the yield curve for such bonds is many hundreds of basis points above the swap yield curve. When the yield curves are this far apart, the result-ant factor sensitivities would be sufficiently different to warrant the use of an additional yield curve.

The result of this is that there are typically 64 factor sensitivi-ties to be calculated for a portfolio of interest rate instruments. These are calculated for a one basis point increase in yield at each of the 15 points on each of four yield curves, as well as for a one basis point parallel shift in each of the four yield curves. The four yield curves are the government yield curve, the money market yield curve, the swap yield curve and a corporate yield curve for non-investment-grade corporate bonds.

Table 5.11 shows the results of a typical factor sensitivity calcu-lation using three of these yield curves, for a swap portfolio, or swap warehouse, that does not deal with non-investment-grade counterparties. This is a small portfolio of swaps that are hedged with government bonds and forward rate agreements.

Table 5.11   GBP swap warehouse

Month	Govt	Money market	Swaps	Govt	Money market	Swaps	Net
1	7.5000	8.2500	8.5000	0	(77)	(2)	(79)
2	7.5150	8.3750	8.5625	0	0	(3)	(3)
3	7.5300	8.5000	8.5625	(1)	0	(10)	(11)
6	7.8900	8.8750	8.9375	2	14	(14)	2
9	8.0850	9.0000	9.0625	20	10	(220)	(190)
12	8.2800	9.1250	9.1875	52	726	(499)	279
18	8.4800	9.2750	9.3125	75	229	(90)	214
24	8.6800	9.4300	9.4300	2,165	0	(2,343)	(178)
36	8.7800	9.5700	9.5700	471	0	(375)	96
48	8.8600	9.6400	9.6400	(240)	0	620	380
60	8.9400	9.6400	9.7000	9,474	0	(9,618)	(144)
84	9.1000	9.6400	9.8600	(850)	0	679	(171)
120	9.2200	9.6400	9.9800	(24,258)	0	24,326	68
240	9.2200	9.6400	9.9800	0	0	0	0
360	9.2200	9.6400	9.9800	0	0	0	0
Total				(13,084)	902	12,446	264

The first column gives the point on the maturity grid in months, from one month out to 30 years. The next three columns show the yield-to-maturity for each of the three yield curves that are needed to value this portfolio – the government yield curve, the money market yield curve and the swap yield curve. The government yield curve runs from 7.5% at one month to 9.22% at 30 years. The money market yield curve runs from 8.25% to 9.64% at four years, and, as there are no cash flows beyond 4 years, the 4-year rate is simply repeated out to 30 years. The swap yield curve runs from 8.5% to 9.98% at 10 years, and, as there are no cash flows beyond 10 years, making interest rates beyond this point are irrelevant, the 10- year rate is simply repeated at all points out to 30 years. Note that this replication beyond the last relevant tenor could lead to faulty valuations if cash flows at longer tenors were to be added at a later point.

The first set of factor sensitivity numbers, running from 0 to (24,258), gives the change in the market value of the portfolio for a one basis point increase in the government yield-to-maturity rate at that tenor. For example, if the 10 year government yield were to increase from 9.22% to 9.23%, then the value of the portfolio would decrease by 24,258.

The factor sensitivity numbers in the Money market column, running from (77) to 229, give the change in the market value of the portfolio for a one basis point increase in the money market yield-to-maturity rate.

The factor sensitivity numbers in the column labelled Swaps, running from (2) to 24,326, give the change in the market value of the portfolio for a one basis point increase in the swap yield-to-maturity rate.

The factor sensitivity numbers in the Net column, running from (79) to 68, are simply the sum of the three factor sensitivity numbers in the row. Thus, these numbers represent the change in the value of the portfolio if all three yields at that tenor were to be increased by one basis point. For example, if the government yield were to increase from 9.22% to 9.23% and the swap yield were to increase from 9.98% to 9.99%, then the value of the portfolio would increase by 67 – the government bonds would decrease in value by 24,258, but this would be more than offset by an increase of

24,326 in the value of the swaps. This is because the holding of 10-year government bills was adjusted so that it would have approximately equal and opposite factor sensitivity to the holding of 10-year swaps. This is done at all points of the yield curve, except that, at the short end, the swaps are hedged with holdings of forward rate agreements rather than government bills.

These yield curve factor sensitivities can be used to evaluate the effect of changes in the slope of all yield curves, such as a steepening or a flattening, or even a twisting in the yield curves.

The totals given at the foot of the table represent the change in the value of the portfolio if every yield on the corresponding yield curve were to be increased by one basis point. For example, the portfolio would decrease in value by 13,084 if the entire government yield curve were to be increased by one basis point. This figure is not exactly the same as the total of all the numbers in the column above, as it has been calculated from scratch. The small difference represents the non-linearity of the factor sensitivity calculation – the effect of increasing a yield by one basis point is not exactly twice the effect of increasing a yield by one half of a basis point.

The total figure in the Net column shows that the entire portfolio would increase in value by 264 if all points on all three yield curves were to be increased by one basis point. The fact that this is a small figure demonstrates that the portfolio of swaps has been fairly well hedged, and that it is therefore almost immune to changes in the overall level of rates. Therefore, this is the most useful single figure in the matrix, because it is not uncommon for the level of interest rates to move significantly.

However, the total factor sensitivity figures at the foot of each column are also important, as they indicate the sensitivity of the portfolio to a parallel shift in a given interest rate curve. The risk of one yield curve moving relative to another yield curve is defined as the basis risk of the portfolio. It is not unusual for the basis between two yield curves to change, especially as a result of changed perceptions of the credit risk of non-governmental securities.

5.2 Managing a Swap Portfolio

Using all these techniques, the factor sensitivity of a portfolio can be calculated, and the results displayed in a convenient format.

5.2.1 The Risk in a Swap Portfolio

These principles are best demonstrated by using them to manage a small swap warehouse. This warehouse contains only two swaps which are hedged with four government bonds. The six positions are listed in Table 5.12 for reference purposes. The assumed current date is 30/9/95. All the factor sensitivities of this warehouse can be determined using the appropriate yield curves. The results are shown in Table 5.13

Table 5.12   Transactions in warehouse

Book	Maturity	Rate (%)	Notional
Swap	30/6/2000	9.50	30,000,000
Swap	31/7/2005	10.00	(40,000,000)
Govt	15/8/1999	8.75	(6,000,000)
Govt	15/8/2000	9.00	(25,000,000)
Govt	15/8/2002	9.00	1,000,000
Govt	15/8/2005	9.25	39,000,000

Table 5.13   Swap Warehouse

Month	Factor sensitivity		
	Govt	Swap	Net
3	(2)	(7)	(9)
6	1	5	6
12	1	6	7
24	0	8	8
36	76	13	89
48	2,287	(1,749)	538
60	9,474	(9,618)	(144)
84	(860)	679	(181)
120	(24,897)	24,326	(571)
Total	(13,913)	13,658	(255)

Table 5.14   Swap warehouse: change in level of rates

Month	Factor sensitivities			Change in yield	
	Govt	Swap	Net	Basis points	Effect
3	(2)	(7)	(9)	10	(90)
6	1	5	6	10	60
12	1	6	7	10	70
24	0	8	8	10	80
36	76	13	89	10	890
48	2,287	(1,749)	538	10	5,380
60	9,474	(9,618)	(144)	10	(1,440)
84	(860)	679	(181)	10	(1,810)
120	(24,897)	24,326	(571)	10	(5,710)
Total	(13,913)	13,658	(255)		(2,570)

Table 5.15   Swap warehouse: yield curves steepen

Month	Factor sensitivities			Change in yield	
	Govt	Swap	Net	Basis points	Effect
3	(2)	(7)	(9)	−5	45
6	1	5	6	−5	(30)
12	1	6	7	−5	(35)
24	0	8	8	−5	(40)
36	76	13	89	−5	(445)
48	2,287	(1,749)	538	−5	(2,690)
60	9,474	(9,618)	(144)	5	(720)
84	(860)	679	(181)	5	(905)
120	(24,897)	24,326	(571)	5	(2855)
Total	(13,913)	13,658	(255)		(7,675)

This format is an extremely convenient one for analysing the effect of various changes in yield curves on the value of the warehouse. The first example is a simple one, in which every interest rate on every yield curve is assumed to increase by 10 basis points. The effect can be calculated by multiplying the total factor sensitivity to a one basis point increase (255) by 10 to obtain (2,550). This means that a 10 basis point parallel shift in interest rates will result in a loss of 2,550. An alternative derivation would be to multiply the factor sensitivity at each point on the yield curve by 10, and then to sum the results to give the total change (Table 5.14).

The result is a loss of 2,570, which is not exactly the same as the loss of 2,550 in the previous calculation. This is due not only to the fact that the numbers have been rounded to be integers, but also to the fundamental non-linearities in the calculation. Although this is a more cumbersome method, it can be readily adapted to any required change in the yield curve. Let us take as an example a five basis point decrease at the short end of the yield curve, and a five basis point increase at the long end of the yield curve (Table 5.15).

In this example the yield curve has steepened, with the long end increasing by 10 basis points relative to the short end. As a result the loss has increased to 7,675. In practice, the trader can use an analysis such as this to estimate the effect of any change in the yield curve, whether it be a change that has already occurred, or a possible change that might occur.

In the above examples, it has been assumed that a change in interest rates at a given point on the yield curve will apply equally to the government yield curve and the swap yield curve. This is by no means always the case. So let us examine the effect of a reduction in the spread between the two yield curves by two basis points. This can be done by multiplying the factor sensitivity to each yield on the swap yield by minus two (-2) and then summing the results (Table 5.16).

The result of this two basis point narrowing of the spread between the two yield curves is a loss of 27,326. A simpler method uses the factor sensitivity to a parallel shift in the swap yield curve, 13,658, multiplying it by minus two (-2) to obtain a loss of 27,316. Again the numbers do not agree exactly due to roundings and non-linearities. The more cumbersome method can be easily

Table 5.16 Swap warehouse: basis risk

Month	Factor sensitivities			Change in yield	
	Govt	Swap	Net	Basis points	Effect
3	(2)	(7)	(9)	-2	14
6	1	5	6	-2	(10)
12	1	6	7	-2	(12)
24	0	8	8	-2	(16)
36	76	13	89	-2	(26)
48	2,287	(1,749)	538	-2	3,498
60	9,474	(9,618)	(144)	-2	19,236
84	(860)	679	(181)	-2	(1,358)
120	(24,897)	24,326	(571)	-2	(48,652)
Total	(13,913)	13,658	(255)		(27,326)

Table 5.17   Swap warehouse: non-parallel basis risk

Month	Factor sensitivities			Change in yield	
	Govt	Swap	Net	Basis points	Effect
3	(2)	(7)	(9)	2	(14)
6	1	5	6	2	10
12	1	6	7	2	12
24	0	8	8	2	16
36	76	13	89	2	26
48	2,287	(1,749)	538	2	(3,498)
60	9,474	(9,618)	(144)	2	(19,236)
84	(860)	679	(181)	–2	(1,358)
120	(24,897)	24,326	(571)	–2	(48,652)
Total	(13,913)	13,658	(255)		(72,694)

adapted to estimate the effect of different changes in the spread, such as an increase of two basis points in the spread at the short end of the yield curve and a decrease of two basis points in the spread at the long end (Table 5.17).

The overall loss has now increased to 72,694 by having different changes in the spread at different points in the yield curve.

However, there are combinations of relatively small changes that can produce even greater losses than this. Let us again calculate the effect of changing each point on each yield curve by only two basis points, but in this case, let us make the change in whatever direction causes a loss. This means that the spreads at the longer tenors change by four basis points (Table 5.18).

These relatively small changes – two basis points is not an uncommon change in interest rates from day to day, nor is four ba-

Table 5.18   Swap warehouse: worst case basis risk

Month	Factor sensitivities			Change in yield	
	Govt	Swap	Net	Basis points	Effect
3	(2)	(7)	(9)	+2/+2	(18)
6	1	5	6	–2/–2	(10)
12	1	6	7	–2/–2	(14)
24	0	8	8	–2/–2	(16)
36	76	13	89	–2/–2	(178)
48	2,287	(1,749)	538	–2/+2	(18,072)
60	9,474	(9,618)	(144)	–2/+2	(38,184)
84	(860)	679	(181)	+2/–2	(13,078)
120	(24,897)	24,326	(571)	+2/–2	(98,446)
Total	(13,913)	13,658	(255)		(148,016)

sis points an unlikely change in spread – can result in extremely large losses, in this case a loss of 148,016. Although the original hedging transactions worked exceedingly well at hedging the warehouse against a parallel shift in interest rates, there is still considerable risk arising from yield curve risk and basis risk. These risks must be monitored continuously by the trader responsible for running such a warehouse, and every attempt made to reduce the exposure to acceptable levels. Some of the techniques used by the trader are demonstrated in Section 5.2.2.

5.2.2 Managing an Interest Rate Swap Portfolio

The first step is to know the approximate factor sensitivity of new transactions, which is usually expressed as an amount per million of face value. Table 5.19 shows these factor sensitivities calculated using the coupon rates implied by the yield curves, in other words, for on-market transactions.

Using these factor sensitivities, an equivalent portfolio can be found. This is done by dividing the factor sensitivity at each point on the maturity grid by the factor sensitivity of an on-market instrument. The equivalent portfolio is that portfolio of swaps and government bonds which has the same sensitivity to changes in interest rates as the entire warehouse .

In Table 5.20, the equivalent portfolio is only shown to the nearest million of face value. Note that we divided by the negative of the factor sensitivity in Table 5.19, because a long position has a negative factor sensitivity. For this simple case, the equivalent

Table 5.19   Factor sensitivity of 1,000,000 on-market deals

Month	Factor sensitivities	
	Govt	Swap
24	181	179
36	259	256
48	332	326
60	398	390
84	512	500
120	649	628

Table 5.20   Swap warehouse

Month	Factor sensitivity		Factor sensitivity (per million)		Equivalent portfolio	
	Govt	Swap	Govt	Swap	Govt	Swap
3	(2)	(7)				
6	1	5				
12	1	6				
24	0	8				
36	76	13				
48	2,287	(1,749)	–332	–326	–7	5
60	9,474	(9,618)	–398	–390	–24	25
84	(860)	679	–512	–500	2	–1
120	(24,897)	24,326	–649	–628	38	–39
Total	(13,913)	13,658				

portfolio can be compared to our original portfolio, which had government bonds with face values of –6, –25, +1 and +39, as well as swaps with notional values of +30 and –40. Essentially, the above analysis has simply re-allocated the notional amounts that fall between the points on the maturity grid to the nearest points on the maturity grid.

With this information, the swap trader can now attempt to balance the warehouse, thereby reducing the fairly high level of basis risk. To do this, the trader requires a 5 million short four-year swap, a 25 million short five-year swap, a 1 million long seven-year swap and a 39 million long ten-year swap. Clearly this calculation does not depend upon the exact factor sensitivities of on-market deals; the use of 400 for a five-year transaction rather than 390 would have resulted in the same trades. Such trades will be more likely if the trader changes the current bid and offers quotes to encourage counterparties to transact the appropriate swaps.

For example, short five-year swaps are required, with total notionals of 25 million. The mid-point five-year swap rate is currently 9.7%, so let us assume that the bid/offer quotes are 9.6%/9.8%. A short swap is one in which the institution will pay fixed rates and receive floating rates. If the current bid/offer quotes are 9.6%/9.8%, then the institution is prepared to pay a fixed rate of 9.6% on a short swap and wants to receive a fixed rate of 9.8% on a long swap. By changing this quote to 9.7%/9.9%, the chance of transacting a short swap is increased, as the counterparty will receive a higher rate of 9.7% when the rest of the market is only paying 9.6%. Similarly, the chance of transacting a long swap is decreased, as the counterparty would have to pay the higher rate of 9.9% when the rest of the market is prepared to receive only 9.8%. If some counterparty really wants to enter into a long swap at 9.9%, then the trader will probably deal and use some of the extra profit to subsidise another counterparty into a short swap by quoting 9.75%/9.95%.

When such trading techniques are used, care should be taken to ensure that there is sufficient liquidity in the market for the flow of transactions to continue. Otherwise, the institution will be left with a dramatically mismatched warehouse, thereby being exposed if there were to be a major movement in interest rates.

In the above example, it is more likely that a market-maker will change their market quote from 9.6%/9.8% to 9.6%/9.9%. In this way, the short swap remains unchanged and is therefore still competitive with the market, but the long swap is now expensive compared with the rest of the market, and so counterparties will be discouraged from entering into long swap transactions.

The factor sensitivity of an on-market transaction does depend upon the exact level of interest rates, and so the factor sensitivity of swaps and government bonds were slightly different in Table 5.19. This means that a swap warehouse that is suitably hedged with government bonds today is extremely unlikely to remain hedged until all the swap contracts mature. The purpose of hedging is to keep the warehouse insensitive to changes in the overall level of interest rates, and, as far as possible, insensitive to changes in the shapes of the yield curves as well. Basis risk is not removed by hedging, but by matching the swap book itself, as discussed in previous paragraphs.

Let us examine how a trader can hedge a swap warehouse when a new swap trade is executed. Assume that the starting warehouse is the same as that used in the previous examples, and that a new long four-year swap is executed with a notional value of 2,000,000. Such a swap has a factor sensitivity of negative 326 per million of notional, so the factor sensitivity added to the warehouse is negative 652. This results in the factor sensitivities shown

Table 5.21　Swap warehouse with new four-year swap

Month	Factor sensitivity			New deals		Result
	Govt	Swap	Net	Govt	Swap	Net
3	(2)	(7)	(9)			(9)
6	1	5	6			6
12	1	6	7			7
24	0	8	8			8
36	76	13	89			89
48	2,287	(1,749)	538		(652)	(114)
60	9,474	(9,618)	(144)			(144)
84	(860)	679	(181)			(181)
120	(24,897)	24,326	(571)			(571)
Total	(13,913)	13,658	(255)		(652)	(907)

in Table 5.21.

In Table 5.21, the factor sensitivity of the existing warehouse is shown together with the factor sensitivity of the new transaction. These are then simply added to obtain the resultant factor sensitivity. This is an accurate representation if the new swap is a simple on-market bullet payment swap, but it is also a reasonable approximation if the new swap is off-market with an up-front payment covering the difference.

The total factor sensitivity has increased from negative 255 to negative 907. The new four-year long swap has now to be hedged in order to reduce this total factor sensitivity. A 2 million long four-year swap, with a factor sensitivity of negative 652, can be hedged fairly well by a 2 million short government position, with a factor sensitivity of 664. However, the addition of the four-year swap to the warehouse had a beneficial effect on the factor sensitivity to four-year interest rates, reducing it from positive 538 to negative 114. If 664 were added back by taking a short position in four-year government bonds, then the four-year factor sensitivity would be taken back up to 550. Thus it would be preferable to hedge the new four-year swap at a different point on the yield curve, and an examination of the matrix shows that a 1 million position in 10-year government bonds would be a better course of action. (Table 5.22)

Not only has the four-year factor sensitivity been reduced from 538 to 114, but the 10-year factor sensitivity has been reduced

Table 5.22   Swap warehouse with government hedge

Month	Factor sensitivity			New deals		Result
	Govt	Swap	Net	Govt	Swap	Net
3	(2)	(7)	(9)			(9)
6	1	5	6			6
12	1	6	7			7
24	0	8	8			8
36	76	13	89			89
48	2,287	(1,749)	538		(652)	(114)
60	9,474	(9,618)	(144)			(144)
84	(860)	679	(181)			(181)
120	(24,897)	24,326	(571)	649		78
Total	(13,913)	13,658	(255)	649	(652)	(258)

from 571 to 78. In making this statement, the signs of the factor sensitivity have been ignored, as it is the absolute value that is important, because the direction of any possible movement in the future is unknown.

The total factor sensitivity is now back to 258. If the trader really wants to hedge the total interest rate risk, he can buy a three-year 1 million government bond. This has a factor sensitivity of 259 (Table 5.23).

The resultant total factor sensitivity is now only 1. Although this may appear to be a contrived example, there have been occasions when the author has seen single-digit total factor sensitivities in very large swap warehouses containing swaps with notionals running into tens of billions.

Table 5.23   Swap warehouse with final hedge

Month	Factor sensitivity			New deals		Result
	Govt	Swap	Net	Govt	Swap	Net
3	(2)	(7)	(9)			(9)
6	1	5	6			6
12	1	6	7			7
24	0	8	8			8
36	76	13	89	259		348
48	2,287	(1,749)	538		(652)	(114)
60	9,474	(9,618)	(144)			(144)
84	(860)	679	(181)			(181)
120	(24,897)	24,326	(571)	649		78
Total	(13,913)	13,658	(255)	908	(652)	1

It should again be stressed that the very small total factor sensitivity does not mean that this warehouse is free of interest rate risk. It is immune to parallel shifts in the yield curves, provided that the two yield curves move together. It is still subject to differential moves in the two yield curves, as demonstrated earlier in this section.

5.2.3 Managing a Cross-Currency Swap Portfolio

The above analysis covered the interest rate risk in a single currency only. This becomes a little more complicated when multiple currencies are involved.

Let us next examine a small portfolio of fixed/fixed cross-currency swaps and their associated hedge transactions; namely gilts, treasuries, forward rate agreements and forward foreign exchange contracts. These cross-currency swaps are all between pounds sterling and US dollars. This total portfolio is then analysed one currency at a time.

Firstly, the factor sensitivities to changes in the US dollar yield curve are calculated. The results are shown in Table 5.24.

The three yield curves used to revalue the different instruments

Table 5.24   Factor sensitivities of swap warehouse: US dollars

Month	Yield curves			Factor sensitivities			
	Govt	Money market	Swaps	Govt	Money market	Swaps	NET
1	7.5300	8.2500	8.5625	0	0	0	0
2	7.5300	8.3750	8.5625	0	0	0	0
3	7.5300	8.5000	8.5625	0	0	(17)	(18)
6	7.8900	8.8750	8.9375	16	0	(6)	10
9	8.0850	9.0000	9.0625	(1)	0	(46)	(47)
12	8.2800	9.1250	9.1875	17	38	(264)	(209)
18	8.4800	9.2750	9.3088	209	88	(944)	(647)
24	8.6800	9.4300	9.4300	2,545	481	(1,349)	1,676
36	8.7800	9.5700	9.5700	690	(564)	20	146
48	8.8600	9.6400	9.6400	(53)	(2,054)	583	(1,524)
60	8.9400	9.6400	9.7000	7,745	2,886	(9,205)	1,425
84	9.1000	9.6400	9.8600	(3,062)	376	2,611	(75)
120	9.2200	9.6400	9.9800	(24,387)	(2,568)	26,079	(876)
180	9.2200	9.6400	10.000	0	0	0	0
240	9.2200	9.6400	10.000	0	0	0	0
360	9.2200	9.6400	10.000	0	0	0	0
Whole yield curve + 1 basis point				(16,275)	(1,318)	17,455	(139)
Spot FX 1% Sensitivity in GBP US dollars			1.500	35,693	4,631	(42,027)	(1,703)

Table 5.25   Factor sensitivities of swap warehouse: pound sterling

Month	Yield curves			Factor sensitivities			NET
	Govt	Money market	Swaps	Govt	Money market	Swaps	
1	7.0000	7.1500	7.5000	0	76	0	76
2	7.0000	7.2000	7.5000	0	0	(1)	(1)
3	7.0000	7.2500	7.5000	3	0	12	16
6	7.1000	7.3000	7.6000	(8)	(9)	(13)	(30)
9	7.1500	7.4000	7.6500	9	(10)	33	32
12	7.2000	7.5000	7.7000	(9)	(823)	509	(323)
18	7.2500	7.5500	7.7500	(160)	(414)	1,673	1,099
24	7.3000	7.6000	7.8000	(2,194)	(885)	1,995	(1,084)
36	7.4000	7.7000	7.9500	(540)	1,065	(440)	84
48	7.5000	7.8000	8.1000	(2,087)	4,002	(1,585)	330
60	7.6000	7.8000	8.2500	(12,201)	(5,836)	17,997	(40)
84	7.7000	7.8000	8.4000	3,222	(581)	(2,539)	102
120	7.8000	7.8000	8.5000	44,329	5,142	(49,660)	(190)
180	7.8000	7.8000	8.5000	0	0	0	0
240	7.8000	7.8000	8.5000	0	0	0	0
360	7.8000	7.8000	8.5000	0	0	0	0
Whole yield curve + 1 basis point				30,353	1,726	(32,008)	71
Spot FX 1% sensitivity in GBP Pounds sterling			1.000	(433,524)	(11,631)	271,006	(174,149)

in the portfolio are given for reference purposes. The numbers in the swaps column give the change in value in dollars for a one basis point increase in the corresponding swap interest rate.

If all three yield curves move up by one basis point, there will be a loss of $16,275 on the treasury portfolio, a gain of $17,455 on the swaps, and a loss of $1,318 on the forward foreign exchange transaction. The total loss is therefore only $139, because the portfolio has been hedged to remove most of the sensitivity to parallel shifts in the yield curves.

The spot FX factor sensitivity is also given. It shows that the value of the total portfolio will only decrease by £1,703 if the dollar were to increase in value by one per cent against the pound sterling. Thus, we must be net short £170,300 worth of dollars. In other words, the portfolio has been made almost completely insensitive to changes in the foreign exchange rates, as well as to changes in the overall level of dollar interest rates.

Next the factor sensitivities to changes in the pound sterling yield curve are calculated, and the results are shown in Table 5.25.

The portfolio has been made insensitive to parallel shifts in the sterling yield curves, with a total factor sensitivity of only £71 if all three yield curves were to increase by one basis point. The spot FX factor sensitivity is attempting to show the effect of the pound sterling appreciating against the pound sterling, with the results measured in pound sterling, which clearly has no meaning when the currency is the base currency of the institution. However, it does show that the net position of the portfolio is short by 100 times £174,149 or £17,414,900.

The extension of the detailed factor sensitivity analysis to multiple currencies is critical to the entire market risk management process.

5.2.4 Managing a Futures Portfolio

The management of a portfolio of government bond futures contracts follows exactly the same principles as for a swap portfolio. The major difference lies in the treatment of the hedging instrument.

In a swap portfolio the swaps are valued using one yield curve, and the hedging instruments – government securities – are valued using a separate yield curve. Thus the factor sensitivities appear in separate columns in the report and the basis risk is clearly visible.

However, there is also basis risk between a government bond future and a government security. The risk is by no means of the same magnitude as that of a swap portfolio, but it should not be completely ignored. As the factor sensitivities of both government bond futures and government securities are calculated using the government yield curve, only the net factor sensitivity is shown. In order to show the trader the extent of the basis risk, a further report is produced which breaks down the net factor sensitivity to a given yield curve by product code. This allows the exposure to government futures and government securities to be seen separately as well as in total.

There is a further problem with a portfolio of government bond futures, namely the exact rates to which sensitivity exists. This is because the value of the future is based on a notional bond, whereas the actual bond to be delivered on the delivery date is the cheapest to deliver bond. Thus the factor sensitivity of the future could change from that of a 10-year bond to that of a 7-year bond. This is by no means a new problem for traders in government bond futures. The solution depends upon the objectives of the institution concerned, namely on whether physical delivery is likely or whether the institution fully intends to trade out of the position before delivery date.

5.3 Managing Forward Foreign Exchange Portfolios

A similar process to that described above can be used to manage the risk in forward foreign exchange portfolios.

The first table that is required is one that shows the present values of the foreign exchange positions themselves. This can be expressed in factor sensitivity terms or in positions, since the factor sensitivity for foreign exchange rates is simply 1% of the position. For an institution with US dollars as its base currency, a typical table, containing purely illustrative numbers, is shown in Table 5.26.

With a display such as this, the trader can quickly see the position in each currency. The base currency of the institution is given in the first row. Although it is often useful to have the foreign currencies listed in alphabetical order, it is sometimes more important to group related currencies together. The Canadian dollar has a fairly low volatility against the US dollar, so it appears in the second row. If there were any other currencies closely tied to the US dollar, they would appear here also. The three European currencies tend to move together against the US Dollar, so these are grouped together.

Table 5.26 FX portfolio: summary foreign exchange factor sensitivity

Currency	Code	Position USD	Factor sensitivity	
			FX Spot	Interest rate
US dollar	USD	0	0	(21,525)
Canadian dollar	CAD	30,000,000	300,000	11,950
Swiss franc	CHF	(100,000,000)	(1,000,000)	(14,100)
Deutschmark	DEM	(100,000,000)	(1,000,000)	(32,800)
Pound Sterling	GBP	45,000,000	450,000	14,275
Japanese yen	JPY	175,000,000	1,750,000	42,200
Total		50,000,000	500,000	0

Table 5.27   FX portfolio: detailed foreign exchange factor sensitivity

Tenor	USD	CAD	CHF	DEM	GBP	JPY
3	(4,860)	400	(900)	(1,000)	960	5,400
6	(5,700)	(300)	(1,000)	(1,200)	1,100	7,100
9	(8,060)	1,200	(1,200)	(1,500)	1,460	8,100
12	(11,500)	1,500	(2,000)	(2,000)	2,100	11,900
15	13,780	1,300	(2,500)	(4,500)	1,920	(10.000)
18	(6,500)	2,100	(1,200)	(5,500)	1,200	9,900
21	(12,300)	1,500	(500)	(4,500)	1,000	14,800
24	11,015	500	(4,000)	(5,000)	2,485	(5,000)
30	12,000	750	(1,000)	(4,500)	2,050	(9,800)
36	(8,200)	1,000	(300)	(2,300)	0	9,800
48	(1,200)	2,000	500	(1,300)	0	0
60	0	0	0	0	0	0
Total	(21,525)	11,950	(14,100)	(32,800)	14,275	42,200
FX spot in USD		300,000	(1,000,000)	(1,000,000)	450,000	1,750,000

It can be seen that the long position in GBP acts as a partial offset to the short DEM position. This is not a perfect offset, because the GBP and DEM are not 100% correlated. Although the DEM and CHF have a much higher correlation, there are short positions in both currencies, so there is no offset available. The important topic of correlation will be covered in detail in later chapters.

In addition to the factor sensitivities to foreign exchange, Table 5.26 also shows the factor sensitivities to interest rates. These factor sensitivities are the effect of a one basis point increase in all interest rates – a parallel shift in the yield curve. However, it is important for a forward foreign exchange trader to properly monitor and manage the interest rate risk in each of the currencies being traded, which requires a detailed analysis of the factor sensitivity at each point down the yield curve. This is shown in Table 5.27.

The forward foreign exchange portfolio has long and short positions at different tenors in the same currency as well as in different currencies. In order to display these in a simple format, only the net interest rate factor sensitivities are shown at each point down the yield curve. If further details are required, then the individual factor sensitivities to each yield curve in a given currency can be displayed, as was done for a swap portfolio in the previous section. The net interest rate factor sensitivities are shown for six different currencies for an institution whose base currency is US dollars. Because the portfolio has considerable sensitivity to interest rates between one and two years, additional tenor points have been included to assist the trader. The numbers are purely indicative.

It can be seen that there is also significant offset between the interest rate risk in certain currencies. Canadian dollar interest rates do show a reasonable correlation with US dollar interest rates, so the fact that the interest rate factor sensitivities have opposite signs does mean that the risk in the portfolio has been reduced, when compared to one in which these interest rate factor sensitivities have the same sign. Similarly, the positive interest rate factor sensitivity in pounds sterling will be a partial offset to the negative interest rate factor sensitivity in Deutschmarks.

For completeness, the foreign exchange factor sensitivities are also included in this table, as the bottom row in the table. This repetition of summary information does simplify the task of monitoring the risk in the portfolio. Traders can see at a glance the risk in their portfolios, and take immediate corrective action to eliminate any unwanted exposures. It is this ability that makes factor sensitivity such a powerful tool in the management of market risk.

5.4 Foreign Exchange Options

When we consider a portfolio of foreign exchange options, a number of additional complexities are introduced. In the following sections, the valuation formula is given, the various factor sensitivities are shown graphically, the mathematical formulae for these factor sensitivities are given, and the information required to manage an option portfolio is described and shown in tabular format.

5.4.1 Foreign Exchange Option Pricing Model

The Black-Scholes valuation formula for a foreign exchange option is as follows:

$$V = S \ \exp\left(-R_f \ T\right) N\left(d_1\right) - X \exp\left(-R_d \ T\right) N\left(d_2\right)$$

$$d_1 = \left[\ln\left\{\left(S \exp\left(-R_f \ T\right)\right) / \left(X \exp\left(-R_d \ T\right)\right)\right\} / \left\{\sigma\sqrt{T}\right\}\right] + 0.5\sigma\sqrt{T}$$

$$d_2 = \left[\ln\left\{\left(S \exp\left(-R_f \ T\right)\right) / \left(X \exp\left(-R_d \ T\right)\right)\right\} / \left\{\sigma\sqrt{T}\right\}\right] - 0.5\sigma\sqrt{T}$$

where
S is the spot foreign exchange rate
X is the strike price of the option
R_f is the foreign currency interest rate
R_d is the domestic currency interest rate
T is the time to the expiry of the option
σ is the volatility of the foreign exchange rate
and $N(.)$ is the cumulative normal distribution function.

Despite the mathematical complexity of this formula, it can be readily analysed to see that there are now four market factors required for the valuation of this transaction, namely the spot foreign exchange rate S, the foreign currency interest rate R_f, the domestic currency interest rate R_d, and the volatility of the foreign exchange rate σ.

Let us examine the various factor sensitivities of an individual option. For simplicity, we will select a Japanese yen-denominated foreign exchange call option to buy 100 Japanese yen for one US dollar, which was written when there were exactly 100 yen to the dollar. This will allow us to interpret the graphs either as showing percentage changes or as showing absolute changes in yen. The parameters of the selected option are given in Table 5.28.

Using the above Black-Scholes formula, this option has a value of JPY 4.45.

Table 5.28 Option parameters

Parameter	Value
Time to maturity	1 year
Exercise price	100
Spot price	100
Domestic rate	3%
Foreign rate	6%
Volatility	15%

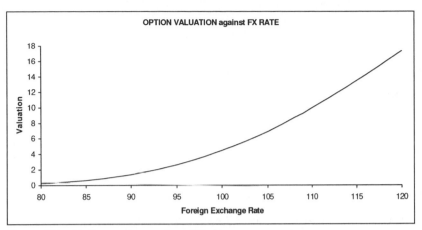

Figure 5.2   Option value against FX rate – one year tenor

5.4.2 Sensitivity to Foreign Exchange Rate

The first factor sensitivity to consider is the sensitivity to the underlying foreign exchange rate. This is calculated by valuing the option using the current spot foreign exchange rate, and then increasing the rate by one per cent, valuing the option again, and then taking the difference between the two valuations. First of all, the value of the option is plotted against the spot foreign exchange rate in Figure 5.2, where it can be seen that the factor sensitivity, represented by the slope of the graph, depends critically on the value of the underlying foreign exchange rate.

In Figure 5.2, the Y-axis represents the value of the option or the premium, expressed in units of the domestic currency (yen), and the X-axis represents the value of the underlying foreign exchange rate. This appears to cover a fairly wide range, namely from 80% to 120% of the current spot value. However, the option has a remaining tenor of one year, and 20% movements in foreign exchange rates over a one-year period are not at all unlikely, especially when it is noted that the option has been priced using a volatility of 15% per annum. When the same option is examined with one month to maturity, the change in the slope of the graph becomes even more marked – the change in slope occurs over a smaller range of values. This is shown in Figure 5.3.

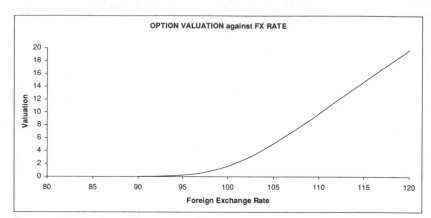

Figure 5.3   Option value against FX rate – one month tenor

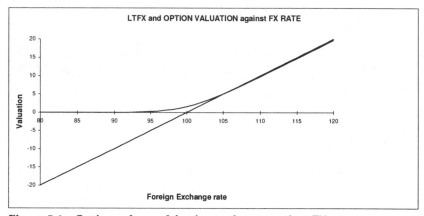

Figure 5.4   Option value and foreign exchange against FX rate

For comparison purposes, the value of a one month forward foreign exchange transaction is plotted on the same graph as the one month foreign exchange option in Figure 5.4.

It can be seen that the factor sensitivity of the forward foreign exchange transaction, as represented by the slope of the graph, is almost constant over the range of values shown, whereas the factor sensitivity of the foreign exchange option changes dramatically.

When the option is well out of the money, it has a value close to zero, and a small change in the underlying foreign exchange rate has very little effect. Thus the slope of the graph is close to

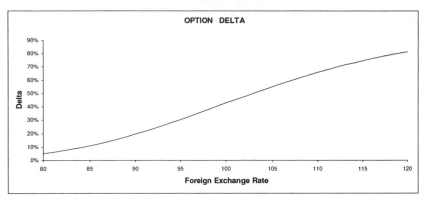

Figure 5.5 Option Delta

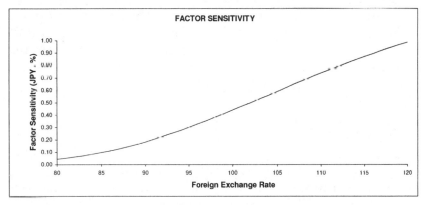

Figure 5.6 Factor sensitivity of an option

zero. In option terminology, the 'Delta' of the option is zero. When the option is well in the money, a change in the value of the underlying results in an almost identical change in the value of the option – the slope of the graph is close to one, or the Delta of the option is 100%. The Delta of the option is plotted in Figure 5.5.

The actual value of the factor sensitivity is shown in Figure 5.6 for the same range of values of the underlying foreign exchange rate. The value of the factor sensitivity is expressed in units of the domestic currency for a one per cent change in the foreign exchange rate.

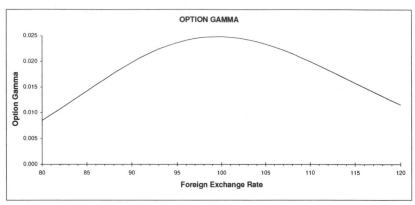

Figure 5.7   Option Gamma

This graph looks very similar indeed to the previous graph in which the Delta of the option was plotted. The Delta of an option is the ratio of the change in the value of the option for a unit change in the value of the underlying instrument. Although this is closely related to the factor sensitivity of the option, it is not exactly the same quantity. Factor sensitivity is the sensitivity to a change in the value of a market factor, and so differs from the Delta when the underlying instrument is not a market factor. In addition, the factor sensitivity is the change in the value of the instrument and is therefore expressed in units of the base currency of the institution, in this case yen. Thus the factor sensitivity includes a multiplication by the nominal value of the contract, which in this instance just happens to be one US dollar. To be precise, the factor sensitivity of an option is the Delta multiplied by the factor sensitivity of the underlying instrument.

Because the Delta of an option changes as the value of the underlying changes, it is useful to have a measure of just how rapidly the Delta actually does change. Such a measure is the 'Gamma' of the option, and the Gamma represents the rate of change of the Delta for a change in the value of the underlying (see Figure 5.7).

For risk management purposes, factor sensitivity limits are placed on the factor sensitivity to the underlying market factor, or on the Delta. However, limits are not usually placed on the Gamma, even though it is important for a trader to know just how sensitive the Delta really is to a change in the underlying market factor. Limits will be covered in detail in Chapter 7.

5.4.3 Sensitivity to Volatility of Foreign Exchange Rate

The next market factor to examine is volatility. The price of an option has an important dependence upon the assumed volatility, and option traders use the term 'Vega' to refer to this sensitivity to volatility. Some authors prefer the term 'Lambda', in order to stay within the Greek alphabet. Figure 5.8 shows how the value of an option changes as volatility changes, assuming that all other parameters remain constant.

It can be seen that the graph is a straight line, which implies that this factor sensitivity is linear, and so it should be relatively straightforward to manage. Unfortunately, such linearity only occurs for at-the-money options. Figures 5.9 and 5.10 show the results for an out-of-the-money (OTM) option in which the spot price is 90, and an in-the-money (ITM) option in which the spot price is 110.

These two graphs show that the factor sensitivity ceases to be a linear function of volatility and acquires a curvature. The dotted straight line has been added only to show this curvature more clearly. One interesting effect is that this curvature is in the same

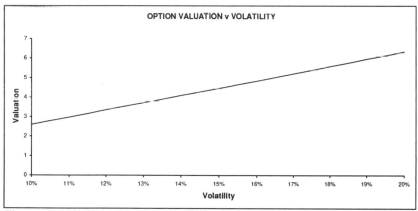

Figure 5.8   Option valuation against volatility

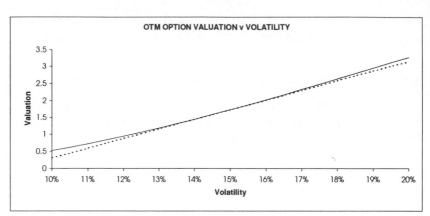

Figure 5.9   OTM Option valuation against volatility

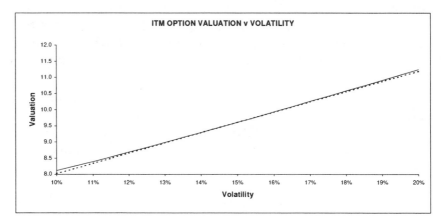

Figure 5.10   ITM Option valuation against volatility

direction in both cases. This has to do with the way in which the term for volatility occurs within the standard Black-Scholes formulae.

5.4.4 Sensitivity to Interest Rates

The two remaining market factors are the interest rates in the two currencies. The factor sensitivities to these market factors are straightforward linear factor sensitivities, for which option traders use the term 'Rho'. One factor sensitivity is positive whereas

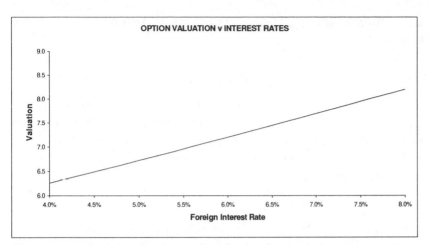

Figure 5.11   Option valuation against foreign interest rate

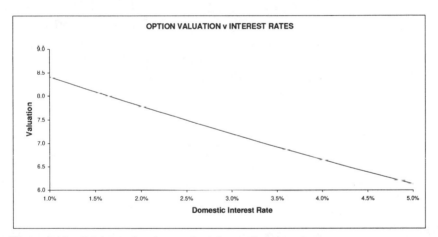

Figure 5.12   Option valuation against domestic interest rate

the other factor sensitivity is negative. They are shown in the two graphs contained in Figures 5.11 and 5.12, in which the value of the option is plotted against the relevant interest rate, so the factor sensitivity is the slope of the graph.

In a similar manner to a forward foreign exchange contract, the factor sensitivities to the two interest rates have opposite signs. The factor sensitivity of the currency that is to be received is negative, whereas the factor sensitivity of the currency that is to be paid is positive.

5.4.5 Sensitivity to Time-to-Maturity

There is one further sensitivity that is used by option traders, and that is the one known as 'Theta.' Theta is the change in the value of the option as the remaining time-to-maturity decreases. Although this is a most important sensitivity, it is not usually regarded as a factor sensitivity, because time is not a market factor. The term factor sensitivity is reserved for those factors that can change unpredictably. Thus, the sensitivity to time is not regarded as a factor sensitivity, because time does not usually change in an unpredictable manner!

The sensitivity of the value of the option to its remaining time-to-maturity is shown in Figure 5.13.

It can be seen that not only does the value of the option decrease as the remaining time-to-maturity decreases, but also that the value decreases at an ever-increasing rate. It is this property of the sensitivity to time-to-maturity that makes Theta a very important sensitivity to be monitored by an option trader.

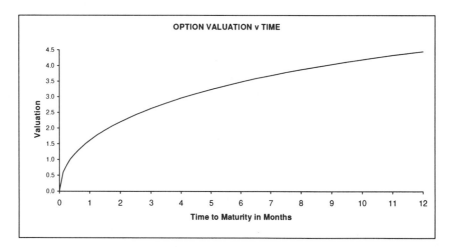

Figure 5.13 Option valuation against time-to-maturity

5.4.6 Mathematical Derivation

The Black-Scholes valuation formula for a foreign exchange option is as follows:

$$V = S \; \exp(-R_f \, T) N(d_1) - X \exp(-R_d \, T) N(d_2)$$

$$d_1 = \left[\ln\left\{ \left(S \exp(-R_f \, T) \right) / \left(X \exp(-R_d \, T) \right) \right\} / \left\{ \sigma\sqrt{T} \right\} \right] + 0.5\sigma\sqrt{T}$$

$$d_2 = \left[\ln\left\{ \left(S \exp(-R_f \, T) \right) / \left(X \exp(-R_d \, T) \right) \right\} / \left\{ \sigma\sqrt{T} \right\} \right] - 0.5\sigma\sqrt{T}$$

where
- S is the spot foreign exchange rate
- X is the strike price of the option
- R_f is the foreign currency interest rate
- R_d is the domestic currency interest rate
- T is the time to the expiry of the option
- σ is the volatility of the foreign exchange rate

and
- $N(.)$ is the cumulative normal distribution function.

From this formula, the various factor sensitivities can be derived by partial differentiation The results are as follows.

The Delta of the option is given by:

$$\text{Delta} = \exp(-R_f \, T) N(d_1)$$

The Gamma of the option is given by:

$$\text{Gamma} = \exp(-R_f \, T) N'(d_1) / S\sigma\sqrt{T}$$

where $N'(x)$ is the normal distribution:

$$N'(x) = \left(1 / \sqrt{2\pi} \right) \exp(-x^2 / 2)$$

The Vega of the option is given by:

$$\text{Vega} = S\sqrt{T} \exp(-R_f \, T) \; N'(d_1)$$

There are two Rhos for the option, and these are given by:

$$\text{Rho}(d) = X\,T\,\exp(-R_d\,T)\,N(-d_2)$$

$$\text{and} \quad \text{Rho}(f) = -S\,T\,\exp(R_f\,T)\,N(d_1)$$

The graphs in Figures 5.5, 5.6 and 5.7 were produced by actually changing the value of the appropriate market factor by one unit and calculating the change in value. The above formulae give the instantaneous change in values, rather than the changes in value over a step of one unit. The magnitude of the difference between the two approaches depends upon the non-linearity of the option, and so is greatest for an option that is near-the-money and is approaching its maturity date.

5.4.7 Managing a Foreign Exchange Option Portfolio

Despite the non-linearity of options, the tools required to manage such a portfolio are similar to those described earlier for a linear portfolio. Let us examine a typical set of factor sensitivities for a foreign exchange option portfolio.

Let us assume that the base currency of the institution is US dollars and the institution deals in options against six foreign currencies – Australian dollar, Canadian dollar, Swiss franc, Deutschmark, pound sterling and Japanese yen. The summary report for such a portfolio would be as shown in Table 5.29.

Unlike a simple foreign exchange portfolio, the factor sensi-

Table 5.29   Foreign exchange options: factor sensitivity summary report

Currency	Spot FX sensitivity		Spot FX volatility sensitivity		Time decay
	US$('000) −1 %	US$('000) +1 %	US$('000) −0.1 %	US$('000) +0.1 %	1 Day US$('000)
AUD	−195.7	164.2	−38.2	35.1	−80.1
CAD	−156.0	165.3	56.1	−55.0	8.2
CHF	725.3	−689.4	0.0	0.0	0.0
DEM	460.2	−600.3	32.5	−36.1	50.3
GBP	−327.2	315.2	37.3	−59.2	29.6
JPY	−2,100.0	1,850.0	153.0	−168.6	−127.0
Total	−1,593.4	1,205.0	270.7	−283.8	−119.0

tivities to changes in the six foreign exchange rates (the Deltas) are shown for both a one per cent increase and a one per cent decrease in each foreign exchange rate. This gives the trader and the risk manager a clear indication of the non-linearity of these options to changes in their underlying market factors. These figures can also be used to obtain an estimate of the Gamma. For example, the AUD option portfolio will show a loss of $195,700 for a one per cent depreciation of the AUD and will show a profit of $164,200 for a one percent appreciation of the AUD. This gives two estimates for the Delta, and thus the change in the Delta (the Gamma) can be estimated to be $164,200 less $195,700 which is a Gamma of negative $31,500 for a one percent increase in the foreign exchange rate.

The second factor sensitivity required for each book is the sensitivity to the volatility of the foreign exchange rate (the Vega). As discussed earlier, this is a linear factor sensitivity for options that are at-the-money, but not for options that are either in-the-money or out-of-the money. Consequently, the factor sensitivity to volatility is shown for both a 10 basis point increase in volatility and a 10 basis point decrease in volatility. These 10 basis point changes are assumed to occur equally at all tenors – a parallel shift in the volatility curve. Although non-linearity is clearly present, it is not as dramatic as the non-linearity in the factor sensitivity to the underlying foreign exchange rate.

Because the time decay of options becomes critical as each option approaches its maturity, the time decay is also shown on the factor sensitivity summary report. This shows the change in the value that will occur over the next day in each book of options, on the assumption that all the other market factors remain constant.

A separate summary report is also produced for the interest rate factor sensitivities, which is in the same format as that shown in Figure 5.26 for a forward foreign exchange portfolio.

However, of more importance for the trader is the detailed factor sensitivity report, one for each option pair, an example of which is shown in Table 5.30.

In this report, the factor sensitivity to volatility is shown at each point down the maturity grid, as well as for a parallel shift

Table 5.30   Foreign exchange options: factor sensitivity detailed report.

Month	Spot FX sensitivity JPY/USD		Spot FX volatility sensitivity		Yield sensitivity		Time decay
	US$('000) −1%	US$('000) +1%	US$('000) −0.1%	US$('000) +0.1%	US$ yield +1 basis point ($'000)	JPY yield	1 Day US$('000)
3			−3.5	3.3	−3.2	3.2	−80.1
6			−2.1	2.2	−1.4	1.4	−25.0
9			−11.6	15.1	−3.2	3.2	−29.6
12			−18.9	20.2	−8.3	8.3	−35.2
15			−5.6	5.6	9.0	−9.0	−8.2
18			20.3	−22.4	−10.3	10.3	9.1
21			50.5	−53.2	−15.7	15.7	14.0
24			54.8	−59.3	8.3	−8.3	13.3
30			29.7	−37.8	6.5	−6.5	8.0
36			39.4	−42.3	−17.4	17.4	6.7
48			0.0	0.0	0.0	0.0	0.0
60			0.0	0.0	0.0	0.0	0.0
84			0.0	0.0	0.0	0.0	0.0
120			0.0	0.0	0.0	0.0	0.0
180			0.0	0.0	0.0	0.0	0.0
360			0.0	0.0	0.0	0.0	0.0
Total	−2,100	1,850	153.0	−168.6	−35.7	35.7	−127.0

of the entire volatility curve. This is entirely analogous to the treatment of the yield curve for interest rates. A normal yield curve is an upwards sloping yield curve, though inverted yield curves do occur from time to time. A normal volatility curve is a downwards sloping curve, because short term volatility is usually greater than long term volatility. This report represents the most detailed factor sensitivity calculations to volatility. However, unlike interest rates, the factor sensitivity to volatility is calculated for both an increase of 10 basis points and a decrease of 10 basis points in volatility at each point down the volatility curve. This is to show the non-linearity in the volatility factor sensitivity. In addition, the effect of parallel shifts up and down in volatility are shown in the Total row. These figures are the ones used in the summary report.

Table 5.30 also shows the factor sensitivity to changes in interest rates at each point down the yield curve. However, the two columns do not show the effect of an increase and a decrease in a given interest rate, but rather show the effect of a one basis point increase in USD interest rates and a one basis point increase in JPY interest rates at each point down the yield curve. In addition, the effect of a one basis point parallel shift in the yield curves are shown in the Total row. These figures are the ones used in the interest rate summary report.

With detailed factor sensitivity reports such as these, the trader is equipped with a powerful set of tools to manage the market risk in an option portfolio. In addition to the tabular presentation above, a graphical presentation is often available, as this can be assimilated far more rapidly. Sample graphs are given in Chapters 8 and 9.

CHAPTER SIX

Statistical Functions

Before considering the market risk being run in any warehouse, it is necessary to define some elementary statistical functions that will be used in the analysis. This is necessary because the past variability of particular market factors is used as an estimate of their future variability.

6.1   Means, Standard Deviations and Confidence Levels

If we have a set of readings of a particular variable, the first two standard statistics that can be calculated are the mean and the variance.

For an array of values X_i, the mean, or average, can be obtained by summing all the readings and dividing by the number of such readings:

Mean $\mu = \sum (X_i) / N$ summed over all i

For an array of values X_i, a reasonable approximation to the variance can be obtained by subtracting the mean from each value, squaring the difference and summing the squares, and then dividing the sum by the number of readings:

Variance $\sigma^2 = \sum (X_i - \mu)^2 / N$

The correct unbiased definition of the variance is only a little more complicated than this approximation:

Variance $\sigma^2 = \sum (X_i - \mu)^2 / \sqrt{N(N-1)}$

The standard deviation is then simply the square root of the variance:

Table 6.1 Mean and variance of daily values

Value	X	X–μ	(X–μ)²
1	8	-2	4
2	8.5	-1.5	2.25
3	9	-1	1
4	9	-1	1
5	10	0	0
6	10	0	0
7	11	1	1
8	11	1	1
9	11.5	1.5	2.25
10	12	2	4
Total	100		16.5
Mean	10	Variance	1.65

Standard deviation $\quad \sigma = \sqrt{\sigma^2}$

A simple example of the calculation of the mean and the standard deviation of a set of 10 interest rates is given in Table 6.1.

The total of the 10 different values of the rate X is 100. Thus, the mean μ is 100/10 or 10.

The total of the squares of the differences from the mean is 16.5, giving an approximate variance of $\sigma^2=1.65$, and an approximate standard deviation of $\sigma=1.28$.

The more exact unbiased formulae will give and $\sigma^2 = 1.74$ and $\sigma = 1.32$.

However, when it comes to measuring price risk, it is not so much the actual values of the rates that are important, but rather the possible change in those rates from day to day. This is found by setting out the rates for each day (X), subtracting the rate on each day from the rate on the following day to obtain the daily change in rates (ΔX), and then calculating the standard deviation of these daily changes. A simple example is given in Table 6.2.

The total of the daily changes ΔX is 0. Therefore the mean μ, which is now the mean of the daily changes, is also 0.

The total of the squares of the differences from the mean change is 16.5, and therefore the variance is $\sigma^2 = 1.74$ and the standard deviation is $\sigma = 1.32$.

This is the standard deviation of the daily change, but volatility is usually quoted as an annual standard deviation. A daily

Table 6.2 Mean and variance of daily change in value

Day	X	ΔX	ΔX-μ	$(ΔX-μ)^2$
0	100	0	0	0
1	101.5	1.5	1.5	2.25
2	101.5	0	0	0
3	100.5	-1	-1	1
4	101.5	1	1	1
5	99.5	-2	-2	4
6	98	-1.5	-1.5	2.25
7	99	1	1	1
8	99	0	0	0
9	101	2	2	4
10	100	-1	-1	1
Total		0		16.5
Mean		0	Variance	1.65

standard deviation of σ_d = 1.32 is equivalent to an annual standard deviation σ_a = 20.94. The method of conversion will be detailed in the following sections.

The **confidence level** is usually expressed in percentage terms. For example, if we are 95% confident that a variable will not exceed a certain value V, then the 95% confidence level of the variable is V. The setting of such a confidence level does not depend upon any assumptions concerning the distribution of the various values of X_i. If we have 1,000 known values of X_i, these can be sorted into ascending order and the 950th value selected. This is known as a non-parametric statistic because no parameters have been calculated for any assumed underlying distribution. However, if we know the probability distribution, then a particular confidence level can also be expressed in terms of the parameters of the distribution. This is discussed further in Section 6.2.

6.2 Normal and Log-Normal Distributions

The next step in examining the changes in market factors is to assign some form of probability distribution to them. Although this is not absolutely essential, it does provide a better understanding of the reasons for choosing certain parameters.

If a series of daily interest rates is taken and the daily changes computed, then these changes can be plotted as a histogram to

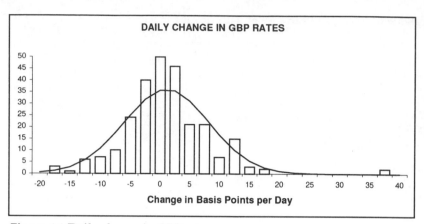

Figure 6.1 Daily change in GBP rates

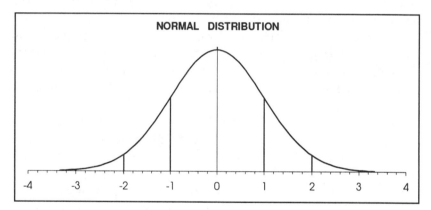

Figure 6.2 Normal distribution

show the frequency of occurrence of particular daily changes. If we examine such a histogram, it will be seen that these rates approximately follow a normal distribution. As an example, Figure 6.1 contains a histogram of the daily change in the GBP one-year money market rate over a 12-month period ending in early 1995, in which the bucket-width is 2.5 basis points.

The shape of this histogram is not dissimilar to that of the standard bell shape of the normal distribution. To demonstrate this, Figure 6.1 also plots a standard normal distribution with the same

Table 6.3 Area bounded by range

Range in Standard Deviations	Area (%)
$-1 < X < +1$	68.3
$-2 < X < +2$	95.4
$-\infty < X < +1$	84.1
$-\infty < X < +2$	97.7

mean and variance as the underlying data of daily changes. Because of the similarity between the histogram of the daily changes and the standard normal distribution, most of the statistical analysis of price risk is done using normal distributions. The differences between these representations are discussed in Section 6.5.

The standard normal distribution is shown in Figure 6.2.

The Y-axis is the probability that the variable will have a particular value. The X-axis is the value of the variable. The scale of the X-axis is in numbers of standard deviations of the variable. The total area under the distribution is, of course, equal to 100%, which simply means that the variable must have some value. It is of interest to record the area under this probability distribution within certain ranges and this is shown in Table 6.3.

If this distribution were the distribution of the daily changes in some market rate, then it is expected that the daily change would be less than one standard deviation for 68.3% of the daily changes — a confidence level of 68.3%. Similarly, it is expected that the daily change would be less than two standard deviations for 95.4% of the daily changes — a confidence level of 95.4%.

If the portfolio has an open position that will result in a change in portfolio value when some underlying market rate changes, then a change in that market rate will normally give a loss if the market rate moves in one direction, and a profit if the market rate moves in the opposite direction. Although risk managers are concerned about unexpected losses, they are not usually averse to making unexpected profits. Consequently, they are only concerned about one side of the above distribution — the side that could result in a loss to the institution. Thus the two standard deviation level of change is regarded as the 97.7% confidence level, rather than the 95.4% confidence level.

As can be seen in Figure 6.2, the normal distribution is a symmetrical distribution. This means that if the distribution were to be applied to changes in interest rates, then equal changes in both directions would have the same probability. For example, if the level of interest rates were 5% at present, then at some future time a rate of 6% would be as likely as a rate of 4%. While this is not unreasonable, the symmetry of the distribution also implies that a rate of 15% would be as (un-)likely as a rate of minus 5%. Intuitively, this does not appear to be at all reasonable. In order to avoid this problem, the normal distribution is usually replaced by the **log-normal distribution**.

With a log-normal distribution, if the level of interest rates were 5% at present, then at some future time a rate of 10% would be as likely as a rate of 2.5%, and a rate of 15% would be as (un-)likely as a rate of 1.666%. Mathematically, this means that rates are as likely to double as to halve; rates are as likely to be multiplied by three as they are to be divided by three. Intuitively, this has far more appeal, especially as rates cannot become negative under a log-normal distribution.

The standard method of defining the log-normal distribution is to state that the logarithm of the daily change, expressed as a ratio, is normally distributed. Adding logarithms is equivalent to multiplication, whereas subtracting logarithms is equivalent to division.

When using a normal distribution, we first ascertain the daily changes as:

$$\Delta X_i = X_i - X_{i-1}$$

and then calculate the standard deviation of the daily changes (ΔX_i).

When using a log-normal distribution, we first ascertain the natural logarithm of the ratio of the daily rates as:

$$L_i = \log(X_i / X_{i-1})$$

and then calculate the standard deviation of these logarithms (L_i).

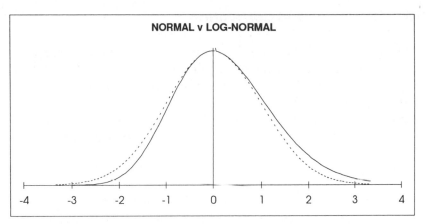

Figure 6.3 Normal *v* **log-normal**

The resultant standard deviation is an estimate of the proportional daily change in rates, not of the absolute daily change in rates. It is therefore a far more relevant statistic in handling financial variables.

The log-normal distribution is shown in Figure 6.3, along with the normal distribution for comparison.

The normal distribution is the symmetric distribution, shown as a dotted line, whereas the log-normal distribution is biased to the right, and is shown as a continuous line. With a log-normal distribution, it can be seen that high values are more likely, and low values are less likely, than with a normal distribution.

Essentially the log-normal distribution is based upon relative changes whereas the normal distribution is based on absolute changes. The use of relative changes is essential when examining, for example, foreign exchange rates. When the exchange rate can vary from 1 to 10 to 100 to 1,000 to 10,000 or even more units of the foreign currency per unit of base currency, a measure of relative change is essential; a change of one DEM in the DEM/USD foreign exchange rate is very different to a change of one ITL in the ITL/USD foreign exchange rate.

6.3 Covariance and Correlation

We now need to define the concepts of covariance and correlation, as these are important for estimating the risk in a portfolio of transactions. To do this, we need to expand on the terms described in Section 6.1.

If we have a set of N values of the variable X_i with mean μ_x, then the variance of that set of values is given by the expression:

$$\sigma_{xx} = \sum (X_i - \mu_x)(X_i - \mu_x) / \sqrt{N(N-1)}$$

The standard deviation of the set of values of the variable X_i is simply the square root of its variance, and so is given by the expression:

$$\sigma_x = \sqrt{\sigma_{xx}}$$

If we have a set of N values of the variables Y_i with mean μ_y, then the variance of that set of values is given by the expression:

$$\sigma_{yy} = \sum (Y_i - \mu_y)(Y_i - \mu_y) / \sqrt{N(N-1)}$$

The standard deviation of the set of values of the variable Y_i is simply the square root of its variance, and so is given by the expression:

$$\sigma_y = \sqrt{\sigma_{yy}}$$

Although these variances indicate the widths of the two distributions, they do not give any information as to whether the two variables tend to move together or not. This important statistic is given by the covariance of the two variables, and is defined as:

$$\sigma_{xy} = \sum (X_i - \mu_x)(Y_i - \mu_y) / \sqrt{N(N-1)}$$

A more common representation of the interdependence of the two variables, X and Y, is given by their correlation, which is defined as:

$$\rho_{xy} = \sigma_{xy} / \sigma_x \sigma_y$$

This definition of the correlation, ρ_{xy}, always results in a number that lies between -1 and $+1$. If the correlation is $+1$, then the two variables always move together in the same direction. If the correlation is -1, then the two variables always move together but in opposite directions. If the correlation is zero, then the two variables are completely independent — information about the directional movement of one variable gives no information whatsoever about the directional movement of the other variable, not even on a probabilistic basis.

The correlation between two market factors is very important when calculating the risk in a portfolio containing instruments whose value depends upon these two market factors. As the risk in such a portfolio will be defined in terms of its variance, we need a formula which gives the variance of the linear combination of two independent variables in terms of the individual variances and their correlation.

Let us assume that we have two sets of measurements, X_i and Y_i, with means μ_x and μ_y and variances σ_{xx} and σ_{yy}. We wish to derive the standard statistics for z, where:

$$z = ax + by$$

The mean of this linear combination is given by:

$$\mu_z = a\mu_x + b\mu_y$$

The variance of the linear combination is given by:

$$\sigma_{zz} = a^2\sigma_{xx} + b^2\sigma_{yy} + 2ab\,\rho_{xy}\sigma_x\sigma_y$$

where σ_{xx} $\left(=\sigma_x^2\right)$ is the variance of X

            σ_x is the standard deviation of X

            σ_{yy} $\left(=\sigma_y^2\right)$ is the variance of Y

            σ_y is the standard variation of Y

and ρ_{xy} is the correlation of X and Y

Let us examine the effect of setting the correlation coefficient to certain specific values.

When the correlation coefficient is +1, the result is that the standard deviation of the linear combination is the sum of the individual standard deviations weighted by their coefficients:

$$\sigma_{zz} = a^2\sigma_{xx} + b^2\sigma_{yy} + 2ab\sigma_x\sigma_y$$
$$= (a\sigma_x + b\sigma_y)^2$$

When the correlation coefficient is −1, the result is that the standard deviation of the linear combination is the difference of the individual standard deviations weighted by their coefficients:

$$\sigma_{zz} = a^2\sigma_{xx} + b^2\sigma_{yy} - 2ab\sigma_x\sigma_y$$
$$= (a\sigma_x - b\sigma_y)^2$$

On the other hand, when the correlation coefficient ρ_{xy} is zero, the result is that the standard deviation of the linear combination is the square root of the sum of the squares of the individual standard deviations weighted by their coefficients. This is the case when the two variables are completely independent of each other. In mathematical symbols:

$$\sigma_{zz} = a^2\sigma_{xx} + b^2\sigma_{yy}$$
$$= (a\sigma_x)^2 + (b\sigma_y)^2$$

By setting a and b to 1 in this expression, we can derive an important corollary, namely that the variance of the sum of a number of independent normally-distributed variables is the sum of the variances of those variables.

These results will be used to aggregate Value at Risk numbers in Chapter 7.

6.4   Determination of Volatility

There are a number of methods that are used to determine the volatility of market factors. The three principal methods are historical, implied and judgmental.

Historical volatility is calculated from a series of historical values of the market factor, such as the quoted daily closing rates. The change from one day to the next is ascertained, and the standard deviation of this set of changes is then calculated using the formula given in Section 6.1. It is important to use daily changes for the estimation of volatilities, as the calculation of market risk will be done over a one-day time horizon. The standard deviation of the set of daily price changes is then annualized to obtain the volatility of the relevant market factor. If two standard deviations are required, in order to obtain a 97.7% confidence level, then this is simply double the one standard deviation number.

The method used to annualize the standard deviation of the daily changes is very straightforward. The annual volatility is simply the daily standard deviation multiplied by the square root of the number of working days in a year. As a formula:

$$\sigma_a = \sigma_d \sqrt{252}$$

This conversion formula is based on three simple assumptions. Firstly, the daily changes in a market factor are normally distributed. Secondly, the change in a market factor on any one day is completely independent of the change on any other day. Thirdly, the volatility of a given market factor is caused by trading in that market factor. The conversion formula can be derived directly from these three assumptions.

As we have already seen, the first assumption is not an unreasonable one, but it is by no means perfect. This is discussed further in Section 6.5. The second assumption is a reasonable one, provided the time horizon is not too long. It should be stressed that there are a number of market factors, in particular interest rates, which demonstrate mean reversion over longer time horizons. The third assumption has been found to be reasonable, in that the changes in a given market factor over a weekend have been found to be not greatly in excess of overnight changes.

Given these assumptions, the ratio of the volatility in any two time periods is the ratio of the square roots of the length of those periods. This follows directly from the fact that the variance of the sum of a number of independent normally-distributed variables is the sum of the variances of those variables, because all the correlation coefficients become zero under the assumption of independence. If each daily change has a standard deviation of σ_d, then the standard deviation over N days is given by σ_N, where:

$$\sigma_N^2 = \sigma_1^2 + \sigma_2^2 + \sigma_3^2 + ... + \sigma_n^2$$
$$= N * \sigma_d^2$$
$$\sigma_N = \sigma_d \sqrt{N}$$

Thus, the ratio of the volatility in any two time periods is the ratio of the square roots of the length of those periods.

An alternative non-parametric estimate at the 97.7% confidence level can be obtained by simply sorting the historical daily changes into an ascending order. If there are 1,000 known values, then the 977th value can be selected. However, the 23rd value would also be at the 97.7% confidence level, but would apply to changes in the opposite direction. There are two methods used to avoid this problem. Firstly, the larger of the two movements can be selected as being the more conservative number. Secondly, instead of sorting the daily changes themselves, the absolute value of the daily changes can be used, which will give equal treatment to movements in opposite directions.

Non-parametric estimates are particularly useful if the historic series contains a few very large daily changes that can be attributed to causes that are highly unlikely to occur again. A few large changes have a dramatic effect on the standard deviation, but are completely ignored by certain non-parametric estimation techniques. This approach should not be used if the causes are likely to be repeated. In such a case, the use of judgmental volatility is necessary.

As an example of a non-parametric estimate of volatility, let us consider the volatility of the Greek drachma one-year money market rate over the period commencing January 1993. A plot of this rate is shown in Figure 6.4.

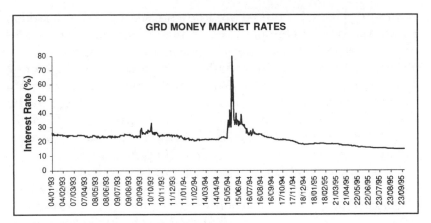

Figure 6.4 GRD money market rates

It can be seen that this series contains just four days on which the interest rate was extraordinarily high, namely 65%, 48%, 80% and 60%. During the period from mid-May to early July, except for these four days, interest rate levels were between 30% and 40%. With 33 months of data, there are 713 data points, and the standard deviation of the daily changes is 237 basis points per day. On this basis, the 97.7% confidence level would be 474 basis points. If the data is sorted into ascending order and the 97.7% confidence level figure is chosen, then 2.3%, or 16, of the data points are discarded. The resultant 97.7 % confidence level change is then reduced to 300 basis points. It should be noted that the five large daily changes associated with these four high interest rates would also be omitted if only one year of data were used.

To be comfortable with such an analysis, an institution must be confident that the factors that led to this major fluctuation are unlikely to be repeated.

Implied volatility is obtained from market quotes for options. The price of a standard option can be calculated from the param eters of the option using the Black-Scholes formula. All the parameters of the option can be readily obtained in the market place, except for volatility. Thus, if the market price of an option is known, the Black-Scholes formula can be used to obtain the volatility parameter that must be used to give the known market price.

The weakness of this method is the fact that all the parameters in the Black-Scholes model are known except for the volatility, and so this one number has to cover many different areas of concern. These include the supply and demand for options, some allowance for the volatility 'smile effect' in which at-the-money options have lower volatility than in-the-money or out-of-the-money options, as well as the approximations inherent in the Black-Scholes model itself. Thus the value of the implied volatility is not really the trader's estimate of expected future volatility, though it still remains a reasonable first approximation.

Judgmental volatility is usually regarded as the last resort. In those markets where there are no liquid options traded, and where historical data is unavailable or misleading, the only method available to estimate volatility is one based on the judgement of the trader or the business manager or the risk manager. This will be the case where there are major discontinuities in the market, such as in the period following a major devaluation of a currency.

6.5   The Validity of Normal or Log-Normal Distributions

Let us return to the question of whether normal distributions or log-normal distributions are good representations for the description of market factor behaviour.

Clearly, the real world does not accurately follow either distribution. Both distributions give a very low probability to very large changes, indeed so low that 'Black Monday' (19 October, 1987) could not really have happened !

Figure 6.5 shows a histogram of the daily change in the GBP one-year money market rate for a 12-month period ending in early 1995.

This figure is typical of many market factors and clearly demonstrates the difference between the real world and a standard normal distribution. The graph that is drawn on top of the histogram is a normal distribution with the same mean and the same variance as the data used for the histogram. The mean is 1.1 basis points per day and standard deviation is 7.1 basis points per day.

When compared to the normal distribution, the histogram has more data points showing small daily changes and more data points showing large daily changes. Consequently, the histogram

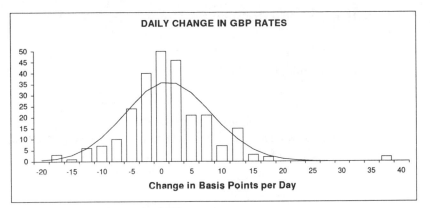

Figure 6.5 Daily change in GBP rates

has less points showing daily changes of about one standard deviation than would be present in a normal distribution. This is a fairly common feature of real world market data.

However, it is of interest to examine the tails of the distribution. With some 250 points in the histogram, one would expect to find 2.3% of them, or about six points, that are more than two standard deviations, or 14.2 basis points, away from the mean of the distribution. In fact, in this set of data, there are seven such points on the left-hand side and six such points on the right-hand side that lie more that two standard deviations from the mean. This is not unusual, and makes the 97.7% confidence level a very useful level to select. The number of points that exceed this confidence level agrees in general with the number predicted by the assumption of a normal distribution, though the amount by which those points differ from the mean is vastly in excess of that anticipated by the assumption of a normal distribution.

This statement should not be interpreted as meaning that the 97.7% confidence level is better than the 97.6% or 97.8% confidence levels, but rather that the two standard deviation confidence level is better than the one or the three standard deviation confidence levels, or perhaps that 97.7% is better than 95% or 99%.

6.6 Constructing the Risk Factor Covariance Matrix

In order to estimate the market risk in a portfolio, it is necessary
to construct a covariance matrix which contains all the market
factors in the portfolio.

The diagonal of this matrix contains the variance of each market factor, and the off-diagonal elements contain the covariances
of each pair of market factors. The matrix is a symmetric matrix,
since $\sigma_{xy} = \sigma_{yx}$. This follows from the definitions given earlier,
which were:

$$\sigma_{xy} = \sum \frac{(X_i - \mu_x)(Y_i - \mu_y)}{\sqrt{N(N-1)}}$$

$$\sigma_{yx} = \sum \frac{(Y_i - \mu_y)(X_i - \mu_x)}{\sqrt{N(N-1)}}$$

Clearly these two definitions are identical.

Just as the variances (volatilities) were estimated using daily
changes in the market factors, so it is important that the
covariances should also be estimated using daily changes. Inci-
dentally, this will usually give lower correlations between many
market factors than would be the case if a longer time horizon
were used. However, this simplification still leaves a very large
number of terms to be calculated. If there are N market factors,
there are N variances and $N(N-1)/2$ covariances.

If we are dealing with 50 foreign exchange rates, then there are
only 50 variances and 1,225 covariances to be estimated. If we are
dealing with the interest rates in these 50 currencies, and there
are 15 points on each yield curve, then we have a total of 750
variances and a massive 280,075 covariances to be estimated.

In order to estimate all these covariances, an automated process is clearly essential. Despite the size of the covariance matrix,
the programming of the calculation is a relatively straightforward
matter. The problem lies in the fact that such a process must be
based on reliable market data, and this can be very difficult to
obtain, particularly when dealing in some of the currencies that

are less frequently traded. One way to ensure that the data is reliable is for the institution to collect and store the data every day, but this requires that a rigorous additional daily process be implemented to verify that there are no obvious errors in the daily market data that is stored for subsequent analysis. One useful test is for the system to check that the daily change is within an expected range, based on an analysis of recent changes.

The system should only allow larger changes to be stored permanently after they have been verified. Even commercially available databases are known to include substantial errors from time to time, which can lead to spurious results.

One bad market rate can give rise to a large increase in the volatility of a particular market factor, since it results in two large daily movements in opposite directions on successive days. This has no effect on the average daily change, as the two large changes offset one another. When calculating the standard deviation of the daily change, every daily change from the mean is squared before being averaged, and so the contribution of one bad rate is out of all proportion.

For example, let us consider the daily change in the GBP one-year money market rate shown in Figure 6.5. This set of data had a mean of 1.1 basis points and standard deviation of 7.1 basis points. Let us assume that just one of the 250 market rates was accidentally increased by 1%, for example from 7.8% to 8.8%. Such an error could easily occur if the data were typed in without verification. This has no effect on the mean whatsoever, because the large increase in the rate on one day is matched by an equal decrease on the following day. However, the standard deviation of the entire set of data increases from 7.1 basis points per day to 11.7 basis points per day — a very significant error indeed.

In addition to the problem of faulty data points, there is the problem of gaps in the data. This could be for a number of reasons. Firstly, the data could have been omitted altogether due to machine failure or human error. Secondly, the data may simply not be available for the particular currency, due to a bank holiday in the country concerned. Such gaps in the data series should be filled before calculating the variance/covariance matrix, if this is at all possible.

One further problem is the complete lack of data for a particular tenor in a particular currency. If the risk management systems have been designed to handle missing tenors, then this problem disappears. However, most risk management systems calculate the factor sensitivities at the same standard tenors in every currency. Thus the variance/covariance matrix must have an entry for every tenor in every currency. This can be solved relatively easily, by simply generating the missing entries from the existing entries.

For example, if there is no market quote for a four-year interest rate, then this rate can be obtained by interpolation between the three-year rate and the five-year rate. The four-year rate is a linear combination of the three-year rate and the five-year rate, and so the formulae for calculating the variance of the linear combination of two variables can be used.

If z is a linear combination of x and y, namely:

$$z = ax + by$$

then the variance z is given by:

$$\sigma_{zz} = a^2 \sigma_{xx} + b^2 \sigma_{yy} + 2a\,b\,\rho_{xy}\sigma_x\sigma_y$$

where $\quad \sigma_{xx} \;\left(= \sigma_x^2\right)$ is the variance of X

$\qquad\qquad \sigma_x \quad$ is the standard deviation of X

$\qquad\qquad \sigma_{yy} \;\left(= \sigma_y^2\right)$ is the variance of Y

$\qquad\qquad \sigma_y \quad$ is the standard variation of Y

and $\qquad\qquad \rho_{xy} \quad$ is the correlation of X and Y.

In order to calculate the variance of the four-year rate, the constants a and b are set to 0.5, the variable X is the three-year rate and the variable Y is the five-year rate. The unknown variance of the four-year rate can then be obtained by substitution in the above formula.

To obtain the covariance of the linearly interpolated four-year rate with other known rates, such as the one year rate, an even simpler formula is used in which the covariance between the one-year rate and the four year rate is the linear combination of the covariance of the one-year rate with the three-year rate and the covariance of the one-year rate with the five-year rate.

$$\text{Cov}_{14} = 0.5\,\text{Cov}_{13} + 0.5\text{Cov}_{15}$$

This is then repeated for all missing rates until the variance/ covariance matrix is complete.

Finally, it is well worth considering the correlations themselves. In theory, every market factor has some correlation with every other market factor. In practice, many of these correlations can be set to zero.

The market factors can be split into eight market factor groups — interest rates, foreign exchange rates, equity prices, commodity prices, and the volatilities of these four groups. Within each market factor group, it is a reasonable approximation to set some of the correlations to zero; this should also be done for any correlation that is calculated to have a small value, less than some minimum. For many institutions, it is also a reasonable approximation to set all the correlations between the groups to zero, which implies that the market factor groups are independent of one another. For example, it is highly improbable that the volatility of the Bulgarian Equity Index would be correlated with interest rates in Paraguay. However, there could well be a not insignificant correlation between the equity index in an export-oriented emerging economy and the foreign exchange rate against the currency of one of its major export markets. Thus some judgement is needed to decide the trade-off between accuracy and simplicity.

If all the inter-group correlations are set to zero, the matrix takes the form of a set of blocks down the diagonal — one blocked matrix for each market factor group. This allows the matrix multiplication to be done in sections, thereby speeding up the process through the elimination of countless multiplications by and additions of zero.

CHAPTER SEVEN

Controlling Market Risk

7.1 Controlling Exposures using Factor Sensitivity Limits

From the definition of factor sensitivity, the factor sensitivity of a portfolio is the change in value of that portfolio for a unit change in the underlying market factor.

Factor sensitivity = Change in value / Change in market factor

$$FS - \Delta V / \Delta y$$

Rearranging: $\Delta V = FS * \Delta y$

Clearly, the management of risk involves limiting the potential losses in a given portfolio. This could be done by placing a limit on ΔV, but such a limit would not be easy for a trader to observe, because it is the product of two quantities, FS and Δy. The first quantity is the factor sensitivity of the portfolio, and, as we have seen, this factor sensitivity can be modified by the trader through the execution of suitable trades in either the major instrument of the portfolio or in the hedging instrument. However, the future change in the market factor cannot be modified by the trader, as this is determined by the market place. Therefore, instead of placing limits on the change in value, which the trader cannot control, it is far more reasonable to place limits on the factor sensitivity, which the trader can control.

As the factor sensitivities of a portfolio can be accurately calculated, they do form a suitable basis for the imposition of limits. A different factor sensitivity limit can be assigned to each market factor, making this an extremely precise tool for the limitation of risk. The size of these limits will be dependent upon the maximum expected change in the market factor. Because the true maximum change could well be an unrealistically high number for day-to-day control purposes, a statistical approach is taken. The 'maximum' change is set to be the change at the 97.7% confidence level – the two standard deviation level.

The factor sensitivity limit is then set to be that level of factor sensitivity which, when multiplied by a two standard deviation change in the market factor, produces a change in the portfolio value that is still acceptable to senior management as the maximum loss that they are prepared to suffer at the 97.7% confidence level – the **maximum tolerable loss**. The probability of exceeding the maximum change in the market factors is 2.3%, which means that it is expected that the maximum tolerable loss would be exceeded once every two months if the factor sensitivity of the portfolio were at its limit. Taking into account the fact that portfolios are not always maintained at the limit, the maximum tolerable loss is usually set at a level corresponding to approximately one month's revenue.

As well as the expected revenue, a number of qualitative factors usually result in adjustments to the maximum tolerable loss. These include the liquidity of the market and the share of that market held by the institution, as well as the experience of the particular trader. It makes sense to give higher limits to an experienced head trader than to a newly-recruited junior trader, all else being equal. This is perhaps the one area where the art of personnel management wins over the science of risk management. Nevertheless, the limits given to such a head trader must not be completely out of proportion to the expected revenue.

Limits are usually set on every single market factor, though it may be worthwhile to have a miscellaneous limit to cover the positions in those market factors that do not warrant an individual factor sensitivity limit. This could well be the case in a foreign exchange portfolio, for those currencies that are rarely traded or are always laid off immediately in the professional market, so that the remaining position is simply the customer spread on the trade.

Table 7.1   Swap warehouse

Month	Govt	Money Market	Swaps	Govt	Money Market	Swaps	Net
				Currency: GBP		**Date : 30-Sep-95**	
1	7.5000	8.2500	8.5000	0	(77)	(2)	(79)
2	7.5150	8.3750	8.5625	0	0	(3)	(3)
3	7.5300	8.5000	8.5625	(1)	0	(10)	(11)
6	7.8900	8.8750	8.9375	2	14	(14)	2
9	8.0850	9.0000	9.0625	20	10	(220)	(190)
12	8.2800	9.1250	9.1875	52	726	(499)	279
18	8.4800	9.2750	9.3125	75	229	(90)	214
24	8.6800	9.4300	9.4300	2,165	0	(2,343)	(178)
36	8.7800	9.5700	9.5700	471	0	(375)	96
48	8.8600	9.6400	9.6400	(240)	0	620	380
60	8.9400	9.6400	9.7000	9,474	0	(9,618)	(144)
84	9.1000	9.6400	9.8600	(850)	0	679	(171)
120	9.2200	9.6400	9.9800	(24,258)	0	24,326	68
240	9.2200	9.6400	9.9800	0	0	0	0
360	9.2200	9.6400	9.9800	0	0	0	0
Total				(13,084)	902	12,446	264

For interest rate risk, there are factor sensitivities to changes in interest rates at all points on all yield curves. However, there are usually fewer limits imposed than the large number that this implies. Let us examine the example of a small portfolio of swaps that were hedged with government bonds and forward rate agreements. Table 7.1 shows the results of the detailed factor sensitivity calculation.

The total factor sensitivity limit for interest rates is a limit on the change in value of the entire portfolio for a one basis point increase in all rates on all yield curves. It is the limit that is placed on the number 264 in the bottom right-hand corner of Table 7.1. For example, the total factor sensitivity limit could be set at 5,000.

The yield curve factor sensitivity limit for interest rates is a limit on the change in value of the entire portfolio for a one basis point increase in all rates at a given tenor on all yield curves. It is the limit that is placed on the numbers in the net column, ranging from –79 to +68. This limit does not have to be the same for each tenor, though it is often set to be the same for all points out to a given maximum tenor. For example, the yield curve factor sensitivity limit could be set at 10,000 for all tenors up to 10 years, and to zero for 20 years and 30 years, if no trades whatsoever are permitted beyond 10 years. A little care must be exercised here, as a trade of 10 years and two days will result in some factor sensitivity appearing in the 20-year bucket, albeit a very small number. If the tenor limit is 10 years from spot, then a very small non-zero limit should be placed on the 20-year factor sensitivity.

The basis risk factor sensitivity limit for interest rates is a limit on the change in value of the entire portfolio for a one basis point increase in all rates on just one yield curve. It is the limit that is placed on the numbers (13,084), 902 and 12,446 in the bottom row of Table 7.1. For example, the basis risk factor sensitivity limit could be set at 20,000.

The basis risk factor sensitivity limit is usually placed on the factor sensitivity of the entire government yield curve. However, it is not unusual for it to be placed on the sum of the factor sensitivities to changes in the money market and swap yield curves, rather than on the factor sensitivities to changes in the individual curves. In the above example, the numbers to be compared against the limit would be (13,084) and 13,348, where the latter number is the sum of 902 and 12,446. This is done because the money market curve is usually regarded as a proxy for the short end of the swap curve: a two-year swap can be replicated by a six-month cash transaction and three six-monthly forward rate agreements.

Other limits could be placed on the numbers in the above table, but usually these three limits suffice. It is of course logically possible to have positions in swaps and government instruments that give zero aggregate factor sensitivities for comparison against all of these limits, while still representing considerable risk to the reshaping of the yield curves in particular ways. This is a matter for the discretion of the risk management policy committee of each individual institution.

In addition, an institution may impose basis risk limits within the same yield curve. This is appropriate, for example, on a futures desk which trades government futures and hedges them with government securities. To do this, the factor sensitivities are split by product type within yield curve – one column for the government securities and a separate column for the futures themselves.

For most market factors, the factor sensitivity limit is an unsigned quantity. A factor sensitivity limit of 10,000 allows the trader to take any position that has a factor sensitivity lying between −10,000 and +10,000. However, there is no reason to prevent the imposition of a smaller positive factor sensitivity limit than the negative factor sensitivity limit. For example, the permitted range could be from −10,000 to +5,000. This form of asymmetric limit is particularly relevant to foreign exchange factor sensitivities, especially in those currencies that are considered to be susceptible to a devaluation. By setting much smaller factor sensitivity limits on the positive side, the institution can limit the loss that will occur if there is indeed a devaluation. For most OECD market factors, the factor sensitivity limits are usually symmetric.

7.2   Definition and Calculation of Value at Risk

From the definition of factor sensitivity, the factor sensitivity of a portfolio is the change in value of that portfolio for a unit change in the underlying market factor.

Factor sensitivity = Change in value / Change in market factor

$$FS = \Delta V / \Delta y$$

or $\qquad\qquad \Delta V = FS * \Delta y$

If the change in the market factor is set to be the change at the 97.7% confidence level, then the change in the value of the portfolio represents the 'maximum' loss that could occur. This value is known as the **Value at Risk**.

The Value at Risk is the amount that will be lost if there is a two standard deviation adverse move in the market factor over the period required to liquidate or adequately hedge the position, provided that this is a minimum of one day.

One day is selected as a suitable minimum to allow for the overnight change in value for those books that are not traded around the clock, even though the one-day volatility is calculated from a series of end-of-day rates. The use of a minimum period of one day also appears to overstate the risk during the day, when the position is being constantly monitored by the trader; if the markets factors were to move in an adverse direction, the trader could adjust the hedge in considerably less than one day. However, this overstatement of the period to liquidate or adequately hedge also compensates for the fact that market liquidity can disappear at exactly the point in time at which the trader wants to hedge the position because of rapidly-changing market rates.

Many institutions calculate the Value at Risk for a daily change in market factors, even for those market factors that cannot be adequately hedged in one day. This is an acceptable approximation only as long as the exposure to those market factors remains relatively small. Even an inadequate hedge will reduce the market risk considerably. For example, the interest rate risk on a particularly illiquid bond with a large credit spread can still be hedged with government treasuries. This will be a hedge against changes in the overall level of interest rates, though clearly changes in the credit spread remain unhedged in such a case.

We have established that : $\Delta V = FS * \Delta y$.

Thus the volatility of the change in value $\sigma(\Delta V)$ is a simple function of the volatility of the underlying market factor $\sigma(\Delta y)$:

$$\sigma(\Delta V) = FS * \sigma(\Delta y)$$

We define the Value at Risk to be the two standard deviation measure of the volatility of the change in the value of the portfolio, or equivalently to be twice the volatility of the change in the value of the portfolio:

$$VAR = 2 * FS * \sigma$$

Because σ is the standard deviation of the change in the underlying market factor, the Value at Risk is the two standard deviation of the change in the value of the portfolio. It is the two standard deviation statistical estimate of the uncertainty in the value of a position, just as the market factor volatility is the one standard deviation statistical estimate of the uncertainty in the change in the underlying market factor. It is important to realise that this Value at Risk number is itself simply twice the standard deviation of a distribution.

This simple formula applies when there is only one market factor to consider. Although the calculation becomes more complex with multiple market factors, the underlying concept remains the same. It is the 97.7% confidence level number representing the amount that could be lost in one day.

With multiple market factors, the change in the value of the portfolio can be obtained from the changes in the values of the individual market factors. With two market factors, a reasonable approximation would seem to be as follows.

$$\Delta V = FS_x \Delta x + FS_y \Delta y$$

and so $VAR = 2FS_x \Delta x + 2FS_y \Delta y$

where ΔV is the change in the value of the portfolio

Δx is the change in the market factor x

Δy is the change in the market factor y

FS_x is the factor sensitivity of the portfolio to changes in x

FS_y is the factor sensitivity of the portfolio to changes in y.

Mathematically, the factor sensitivities are the partial differentials of the value of the portfolio with respect to the individual market factors. Thus if z is a function of x and y, the above formula is equivalent to:

$$\Delta z = \partial z / \partial x \; \Delta x + \partial z / \partial y \; \Delta y$$

which is a reasonable approximation, even though it does ignore all higher order terms including the correlation terms between x and y.

The Value at Risk is the two standard deviation measure of the change in value of the portfolio. To calculate this two standard deviation volatility of the change in portfolio value, we must use one of the techniques already discussed for establishing the volatility of the linear combination of two variables. In order to do this, we must first evaluate the Value at Risk for each individual market factor. When this has been done, these separate measures then have to be aggregated and there are a number of ways of performing this aggregation.

Firstly, a simple addition of each Value at Risk can be performed. Since the Value at Risk of each individual market factor is calculated under the assumption of a two standard deviation adverse move in the market factor, the simple addition therefore assumes that every market factor will move in the adverse direction, namely whichever direction is the direction that will result in a loss. For example, if the portfolio has a long Deutschmark position and a short Guilder position, then the assumption is that the Deutschmark will depreciate and the Guilder will appreciate at the same time. If the base currency of the institution were US dollars, then the two standard deviation change in both European currencies against the US dollar would be about 1.5%. Thus the addition of the two separate Value at Risk numbers implicitly assumes that the Deutschmark will depreciate by 1.5% and the Guilder will appreciate by 1.5%, with the consequent result that the Guilder will appreciate by 3% against the Deutschmark. Given that these two currencies tend to move together against all other currencies, such an occurrence would have an extremely low probability. In fact, the annual volatility of the Guilder against the Deutschmark is less than 3%. In such cases, the result of using simple addition is that the aggregate Value at Risk is dramatically overstated; the Value at Risk calculated in this manner would be at an incredibly high level of confidence.

Secondly, the Value at Risk numbers could be given a sign which is the same as the sign of their factor sensitivities, and then signed Value at Risk numbers could then be added. In this case, the implicit assumption is that the two market factors always move together in the same direction – they are 100% correlated. This approximation will tend to understate the true Value at Risk, especially when market factors do not have a strong correlation.

Thirdly, the two Value at Risk numbers could be aggregated by squaring them, adding the squares and then taking the square root of the sum of the squares. The implicit assumption in this case is that the two market factors are completely independent of one another – their correlation is zero.

Finally, the best method is to take correlation fully into account as the individual Value at Risk numbers are aggregated. For two variables, this can be expressed in a fairly straightforward manner, using the standard theorem in elementary statistics as follows:

If z is a linear combination of x and y, namely:

$$z = ax + by$$

then the variance z is given by:

$$\sigma_{zz} = a^2 \sigma_{xx} + b^2 \sigma_{yy} + 2ab\rho_{xy}\sigma_x\sigma_y$$

where σ_{xx} $\left(=\sigma_x^2\right)$ is the variance of x

           σ_x is the standard deviation of x

           σ_{yy} $\left(=\sigma_y^2\right)$ is the variance of y

           σ_y is the standard deviation of y

and ρ_{xy} is the correlation of x and y.

This definition of the variance of the linear combination of two variables can be used to aggregate the Value at Risk numbers of two correlated market factors. Each Value at Risk number is itself twice the standard deviation of a distribution, since the change in the underlying market factor is a random selection from a (log-)normal distribution. Thus in order to estimate the Value at Risk, we require the two standard deviation estimate for the sum of the two individual Value at Risk numbers.

$$\Delta V = 2FS_x\Delta x + 2FS_y\Delta y$$

where ΔV is the value of the portfolio

         Δx is the change in the market factor x

         Δy is the change in the market factor y

         FS_x is the factor sensitivity of the portfolio to changes in x

         FS_y is the factor sensitivity of the portfolio to changes in y

The variance of this linear combination is given by:

$$\sigma_{vv} = \left(2FS_x\right)^2\sigma_{xx} + \left(2FS_y\right)^2\sigma_{yy} + 2\left(2FS_x\right)\left(2FS_y\right)\rho_{xy}\sigma_x\sigma_y$$

and

$$VAR = \sigma_v$$

The three methods for aggregating Value at Risk, that were described earlier in this section, are special cases of this formula.

When the correlation coefficient is zero, the result is that the two standard deviation Value at Risk measure of the sum is the square root of the sum of the squares of the two standard deviation Value at Risk measures. This is the case when the two market factors are completely independent of each other. In mathematical symbols:

$$\sigma_{vv} = (2FS_x)^2 \sigma_{xx} + (2FS_y)^2 \sigma_{yy}$$

$$= (2FS_x\sigma_x)^2 + (2FS_y\sigma_y)^2$$

Hence $\quad VAR^2 = VAR(x)^2 + VAR(y)^2$

When the correlation coefficient is +1, the result is that the two standard deviation Value at Risk measure is the sum of the two standard deviation Value at Risk measures for the individual market factors:

$$\sigma_{vv} = (2FS_x)^2 \sigma_{xx} + (2FS_y)^2 \sigma_{yy} + 2(2FS_x)(2FS_y)\sigma_x\sigma_y$$

$$= \left[(2FS_x\sigma_x) + (2FS_y\sigma_y)\right]^2$$

Hence $\quad VAR = VAR(x) + VAR(y)$

When the correlation coefficient is −1, the result is that the two standard deviation Value at Risk measure is the difference between the two standard deviation Value at Risk measures for the individual market factors:

$$\sigma_{vv} = (2FS_x)^2 \sigma_{xx} + (2FS_y)^2 \sigma_{yy} - 2(2FS_x)(2FS_y)\sigma_x\sigma_y$$

$$= \left[(2FS_x\sigma_x) - (2FS_y\sigma_y)\right]^2$$

Hence $\quad VAR = VAR(x) - VAR(y)$

For multiple market factors, the extension of the formula above begins to look very complicated indeed, but that is merely a notational problem. By using matrix multiplication notation, the Value at Risk can be specified simply as:

$$VAR = 2\sigma$$

where $\sigma^2 = F M F^t$

    and F is a row vector of the factor sensitivities
                to each market factor

         F^t is a column vector of the factor sensitivities
                to each market factor

         M is the variance / covariance matrix.

This variance/covariance matrix was described in detail in Chapter 6. Both variances and covariances are calculated using the daily changes in the market factors. Because the Value at Risk is the 97.7% confidence level estimate of the change in portfolio value over a one-day time horizon, the variance/covariance matrix calculations must be based on changes over that same time horizon. Over such a short period, many market factors have less correlation than they do over a longer time period. For example, many interest rates tend to increase or decrease together over long periods of time, though they behave almost independently for small changes on a daily basis. Thus it is appropriate for Value at Risk to be calculated using a daily variance/covariance matrix.

If an institution prefers to use the correlation matrix instead of the variance/covariance matrix, this can be done by first multiplying each factor sensitivity by twice the volatility of each market factor to obtain the Value at Risk to that particular market factor. The Value at Risk of the portfolio can then be specified as:

$$VAR = \sigma$$

where $\sigma^2 = V C V^t$

    and V is a row vector of the Value at Risk
                to each market factor

         V^t is a column vector of the Value at Risk
                to each market factor

         C is the correlation matrix.

The multiplication by 2, which is explicitly shown in the formula involving factor sensitivities, is present implicitly within the Value at Risk vector, and so is not shown explicitly.

The effectiveness of correlation in reducing Value at Risk can be seen in a simple example, in which there is a long DEM position and a short NLG position. Assume that the institution has USD as its base currency, and that the factor sensitivity to DEM/USD is 10,000 and the factor sensitivity to NLG/USD is (9,000). If the annual volatility of these currencies is 12%, then the two standard deviation daily volatility will be 1.5%. This gives Value at Risk numbers of 15,000 and 13,500 respectively.

Using the first method – simple aggregation – the Value at Risk is USD 28,500.

Using the second method – full correlation – the Value at Risk is USD 1,500.

Using the third method – independence – the Value at Risk is USD 20,180.

Using the final method – 99% correlation – the Value at Risk is USD 2,510.

Clearly the first and the third methods dramatically overstate the true risk, whereas the second method only slightly understates the risk, because it assumes a correlation of 100%, rather than the true value of 99%.Thus the Value at Risk of a portfolio is critically dependent upon the correlations, or the covariances, between the various market factors to which the portfolio is exposed.

For ease of description, the discussion in the following two paragraphs assumes that all factor sensitivities are positive.

When the correlations are 100%, the Value at Risk numbers to the individual market factors can be added to give the Value at Risk of the portfolio. This gives the highest exposure, as it assumes that all market factors can move by the maximum amount (two standard deviations) in the direction that will cause a loss to the institution. On the other hand, when the correlations are zero, the Value at Risk of the portfolio can be computed as the square root of the sum of the squares of the Value at Risk numbers for each individual market factor.

Clearly the second number is considerably less than the first. There are many market factors between which there is either zero or an insignificant correlation. An institution which diversifies its exposure into a range of such market factors will have significantly less market risk than one which has all its exposure in just one market factor, given that the total risk is the same. This same statement can be made when the second institution apparently diversifies its exposure, but does so into a range of market factors which are highly correlated.

Diversification into highly correlated market factors can be used to dramatically reduce exposure to market risk if the institution has a positive factor sensitivity to one market factor and a negative factor sensitivity to the second market factor. In this case a correlation of 100% would mean that the two exposures completely offset one another. Nevertheless, a correlation in the range 90% – 100% provides an extremely useful method of reducing the total exposure of the institution.

It is not at all unusual for foreign exchange traders to take advantage of these correlations in order to reduce their total exposure in a sensible manner. For example, if a large BEF/USD transaction were to be executed with a customer, the trader would want to lay it off in the professional market. If the transaction were of sufficient size to move the market against the trader, then the trader would not want to lay it all off at once. A sensible method is to lay off as much as possible in BEF/USD and execute the balance in DEM/USD, which is a much more liquid market. The DEM/USD transaction would be unwound subsequently into BEF/USD in such a manner as to leave the market relatively undisturbed. During the interim period, the trader would not have a particularly large Value at Risk number, as the long position in one currency would be a very good offset to the short position in the other currency, given that these currencies show a high degree of correlation.

7.3   Controlling Exposures using Value at Risk Limits

The Value at Risk represents the amount that could be lost under a two standard deviation or 97.7% confidence level. Thus it would appear to be a very useful number on which to set a limit, to ensure that an institution is not exposed to too great a risk, given the expected revenue and the known capital base of the institution.

Value at Risk limits are indeed useful for this purpose. However, their known limitations must be taken into account, or too great a reliance might otherwise be placed on the Value at Risk number. The number is only a 97.7% confidence level number, and is therefore not the maximum loss that the institution could suffer. An institution must not be mislead into believing that the Value at Risk is a maximum loss. In other words, the limit on the Value at Risk does not limit the potential loss to an amount equal to the Value at Risk.

An important assumption behind the Value at Risk methodology is that the volatilities and correlations calculated from historical data will continue to hold for the next day. In general, this is a perfectly satisfactory assumption, but it does break down in periods of high volatility, such as the period surrounding the devaluation of a particular currency. In periods such as this, there would appear to be two alternatives. The first is to increase the volatility of the particular currency in the variance/covariance matrix, which will increase the calculated Value at Risk number that is to be compared against the Value at Risk limit. The second is to decrease the Value at Risk limit, while leaving the volatility of the particular currency in the variance/covariance matrix unchanged, until such time as a new volatility can be established.

However, neither of these is a practical response. In the first instance, it is extremely difficult and not very meaningful to make a significant change to the volatility (variance) of a given market factor in the variance/covariance matrix without changing all the covariances of that market factor. New covariances are required, and these will be calculated using historical data. In the second instance, the variance/covariance matrix should be updated as soon as sufficient data has been gathered to obtain a reasonably reliable new matrix. A trader could reduce the Value at Risk by eliminating positions in other stable currencies and increasing positions in the newly-volatile currency.

The correct response in such a situation is the far more precise one of reducing the factor sensitivities of the particular currency causing concern. This specifically targets that currency, without limiting trading in any other currencies. For this reason, the Value at Risk limits are complementary to the factor sensitivity limits. Both are required in a practical risk management system.

7.4 Relationship between Value at Risk Limits and Factor Sensitivity Limits

When there is only one market factor involved in a particular portfolio, the relationship between the Value at Risk limit and the factor sensitivity limit is extremely straightforward:

$$VARL = 2 * FSL * \sigma$$

In such a simple case, there is clearly no benefit in having two distinct limits. However, this simple approach fails when there are two or more market factors.

The Value at Risk limit attributable to each individual market factor can be calculated using the above formula. These separate Value at Risk limits must then be aggregated in some way. This would appear to be the same problem as that discussed earlier with regard to aggregating Value at Risk numbers, but unfortunately it is even more complex.

The first method is the simple addition of the Value at Risk limits. This assumes that every market factor will be at its factor sensitivity limit in whichever direction will result in a loss to the institution. Clearly the aggregate Value at Risk limit would be dramatically overstated.

The second method is to calculate the aggregate Value at Risk limit by squaring the individual Value at Risk limits, adding the squares and then taking the square root of the sum of the squares. This method assumes that the underlying market factors are completely independent, an assumption which frequently leads to an overstatement of the aggregate Value at Risk limit.

The best method used for aggregating Value at Risk amounts was to employ a variance / covariance matrix against the signed factor sensitivity vectors. This is an appropriate method when these quantities have a sign, but factor sensitivity limits are not signed. Because there is no indication of the direction in which market factors might change in the future, most factor sensitivity limits are the same for both increases and decreases in the market factor. The exception was discussed at the end of Section 7.1.

Consequently, there is no straightforward method of establishing a Value at Risk limit given the factor sensitivity limits of the underlying market factors. This can only be done by setting up typical portfolios in which certain market factors are at their factor sensitivity limits in different directions and then calculating the Value at Risk for the portfolio. When this has been done for a reasonably wide range of typical portfolios, the Value at Risk limit for the given factor sensitivity limits can then be estimated to lie within a certain range of values, from which a suitable Value at Risk limit can be selected.

7.5 Performance Limits

The above limits are all prospective or forward-looking controls. They attempt to control the future potential loss of the institution by ensuring that exposures to all the underlying market factors are within suitable bounds.

The factor sensitivity limits and the Value at Risk limits dictate the maximum size of the position that can be taken by a trader. The limits set on this position are intended to limit the loss that can be suffered in any one day, such that the potential loss is within some reasonable bound. It is feasible for a trader to never exceed these limits, while still losing significant sums every day to the extent that the cumulative losses become intolerable.

Thus, there should also be a separate set of retrospective or backward-looking controls, to act as a warning to senior management. These controls cannot be formal limits, because it is not possible to place a limit on what has already happened. These additional controls are triggers – **management action triggers**.

The management action trigger is a figure, expressed in the base currency of the institution, that defines the tolerance level of senior management towards accepting market risk-related losses on a cumulative month-to-date basis, at a given level of the organizational hierarchy. Clearly, such a control must be monitored every day, which is one more reason why the mark-to-market process must be performed every day.

As in the case of the position limits – factor sensitivity limits and Value at Risk limits – the level of the management action trigger is set as a function of the expected revenue of the business unit, adjusted for the experience of the trader and other qualitative factors. For consistency, the management action trigger should be greater than the factor sensitivity limit times a two standard deviation move in the market factor, as otherwise the management action trigger could be exceeded on the first day of the month, even though the trader was within his factor sensitivity limits. For consistency, the management action trigger should be less than 20 times the factor sensitivity limit times a two standard deviation move in the market factor, as otherwise the management action trigger would not be exceeded even when the trader was at his factor sensitivity limits and the market moved two standard deviations in the adverse direction on every trading day in the month.

The management action trigger should also be set at a lower level than the maximum tolerable loss in a given month. This will mean that breaching the management action trigger will act as a warning to senior management that the actual loss is approaching, and so could exceed, the maximum tolerable loss. There is a case to be made for setting the maximum tolerable loss equal to the Value at Risk limit, so that the management action trigger is less than the Value at Risk limit. Some care must be taken if this is done. Such an equality implies that the Value at Risk limit represents the maximum tolerable loss over any one-month period, as well as representing the amount of risk that can be taken every day at the 97.7% confidence level. Such a dichotomy is difficult to resolve.

There should be a management action trigger at each level of the organizational hierarchy within the trading organization. Conceptually, a management action trigger is assigned to the highest level of the organization, and is then allocated downwards to the lower levels. An organizational level may allocate a greater amount of management action trigger than it receives, provided that the business units at the lower level are in fact different businesses – in other words, their performances are not 100% correlated with one another. The more independence that there is between these business units, the lower the correlation, and so the greater the permissible over-allocation factor. With completely independent businesses, this correlation becomes zero, and the permissible degree of over-allocation is greatest. The level of over-allocation is then indicated by the ratio of the sum of the individual management action triggers to the square root of the sum of the squares of the individual management action triggers.

If the month-to-date loss exceeds the management action trigger, the next level of management is informed immediately. This results in a formal discussion, in order to decide upon the subsequent course of action.

The first action to be taken when the loss of a particular business unit exceeds its management action trigger, is that the management action trigger of the unit is increased to cover or to regularize the excess. This can be simply done by the next level of management, provided that the higher level of management has some management action trigger in reserve. This will be the case if the management action trigger of the higher level has not also been exceeded, because the losses in the particular business unit have been rolled up to that level. Increasing the management action trigger in one of the lower level business units is tantamount to increasing the over-allocation factor. Such an increase remains valid until the cumulative month-to-date losses fall below the original management action trigger. Usually, this is not until the end of the month, when the cumulative month-to-date figure is reset.

If the higher level has also exceeded its management action trigger, then an increase will have to be obtained from the next higher level of management. Thus a large cumulative loss at a lower level can escalate up through the organization, attracting in the attention of more senior management to the problem.

The decision that is taken could be either to maintain the current position, or to close out the current position, in whole or in part, by liquidating the open position, by taking an opposite position in the same market or by taking an opposite hedging position in a closely-related market. The decision as to which course of action should be taken is documented along with the reasoning that led to the decision. This documentation is essential, even when the course of action is to do nothing at all, but simply hold the current positions.

In order to operate the management action trigger process, the cumulative month-to-date losses must be monitored daily. Thus, except in the special case of a single major market movement causing the loss, there should be advance warning that the cumulative month-to-date losses are approaching the management action trigger. Obviously, trading management should have made decisions and taken some action before the management action trigger is actually triggered. The formal process should therefore be regarded as a backstop to the normal management of the portfolio.

In the above description, it is the cumulative month-to-date losses that are compared against the management action trigger. There is a strong case to be made for using the losses over the last month in a rolling one-month period, instead of the cumulative month-to-date losses. Although there is nothing conceptually wrong with such an approach, it does lead to problems in handling breaches of the trigger which lack the simplicity of the method described above.

CHAPTER EIGHT

Non-Linear Market Risk

8.1 Value at Risk Approximations for Non-Linear Portfolios

Most of the analysis in the preceding chapters relates to linear risks. Linear risks occur in those portfolios where the change in the value of the portfolio can be calculated, to a reasonably high degree of accuracy, by the formula:

$$\Delta V = FS * \Delta y$$

where ΔV is the change in the value of the portfolio

       FS is the factor sensitivity

       Δy is the change in the market factor.

The Value at Risk is then given by the formula:

$$VAR = FS * (2\sigma)$$

where VAR is the Value at Risk

         FS is the factor sensitivity

         σ is the standard deviation of the daily change in the market factor y.

Because of the linearity of the underlying market factors, such portfolios are relatively straightforward to control. However, option portfolios are definitely non-linear with regards to their underlying market factors. In option terminology, the approximate formula for the change in value becomes:

$$\Delta V = \text{Delta} * \Delta y$$

given that Delta is in the appropriate units to make the result a value in the currency.

This estimate of the change in value can be a very poor estimate for non-linear option portfolios, especially as the magnitude of Δy increases. In order to calculate Value at Risk, Δy has to be set equal to 2σ, and a change of this magnitude is usually sufficiently large for this to be a poor estimate of the change in value. This estimate can be improved substantially by using the Gamma of the option portfolio:

$$\Delta V = \text{Delta} * \Delta y + 0.5 * \text{Gamma} * \Delta y^2$$

provided Delta and Gamma are in the appropriate units in order to make the result a value in the currency.

This formula is derived by including the second term of a Taylor series expansion of the valuation function about the current valuation, namely:

$$\Delta V = dV / dy * \Delta y + 0.5 * d^2V / dy^2 * \Delta y^2 + ...$$

For further details on the mathematical techniques behind such expansions, the reader is referred to any of the standard mathematics textbooks covering elementary calculus.

The addition of this second term removes the linearity from the above equation, turning it into a quadratic formulation. The most important effect of this non-linearity is that the result of an upwards movement in the market factor can no longer be treated as being equal and opposite to the result of a downwards shift in the market factor. This was clearly shown in the detailed factor sensitivity reports for options in Section 5.4.7. However, another important consequence of this non-linearity is that the matrix multiplication method for calculating the true Value at Risk is no longer valid.

There is, of course, no reason to be restricted to the second differential coefficient in the above Taylor series expansion. If the product system is capable of fitting higher order equations to the risk profile, then these can also be used in order to obtain an even better estimate of the change in the value of the portfolio for a change in the underlying market factor. However, such a methodology is very rarely implemented.

Although the matrix multiplication method for calculating Value at Risk no longer gives an accurate result, it is nevertheless worth retaining the simple matrix multiplication method to obtain a 'linear' Value at Risk. Firstly, such a measure incorporates most of the risk in a typical institution in which options form a relatively small part of the total exposure to market risk. Secondly, in the option portfolios themselves, the Delta approximation is a reasonably accurate method of obtaining the change in the value of the portfolio for a relatively small change in the underlying market factors – this is the case whenever the Gamma is small. In general, one of the prime objectives of an option trader is to keep both Delta and Gamma as small as is practicable.

The variance/covariance matrix multiplication method is based upon the factor sensitivities to a unit change in the underlying market factor. There are a number of different approximations that could be used as the factor sensitivity to the underlying instrument in the case of options. These various approximations can be seen graphically in Figure 8.1, which has been drawn for

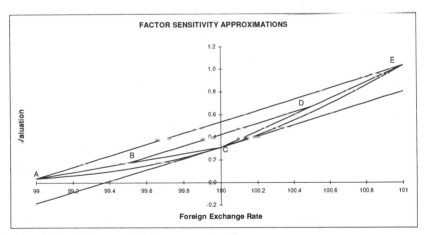

Figure 8.1   Factor sensitivity approximations

an option with one day to expiry, in order to have sufficient non-linearity to clearly show the different approximations.

Firstly, the factor sensitivity that is used for an option portfolio could be the change in value for an increase of one unit in the market factor, as is done for linear portfolios. This is given by the increase in value along the chord CE in the graph.

Secondly, it could be the average of the changes in value for an increase of one unit and a decrease of one unit (with the sign changed). This is the average of the changes in value along AC and CE, which is equivalent to the increase in value along BD. In graphical terms, this average is a good approximation to the tangent to the curve at point C, and so represents a better approximation than using the chord for an increase of one unit in the market factor.

Alternatively, for a wide range of options, there is an analytical expression for the tangent to the curve – the factor sensitivity. This was derived using calculus in Chapter 7. The tangent is the actual rate of change exactly at the current value of the market factor. It also represents a good approximation to the average of the changes from an increase and from a decrease. Since the Value at Risk could come from either an increase or a decrease in the underlying market factor, the average factor sensitivity (derived either from the tangent or from the two chords) will give a slightly better approximation to the true Value at Risk than the use of the standard factor sensitivity.

8.2 Non-Linear Value at Risk

For linear portfolios, the effect of a two standard deviation change can be derived by multiplying the effect of a one basis point or a one per cent change in the market factor by the two standard deviation move in the market factor, expressed in the appropriate units. This gives a result for the Value at Risk that is sufficiently accurate for all risk monitoring purposes.

Because of the non-linearities implicit in option portfolios, this approach is not sufficiently accurate, so some additional methods are needed to calculate the Value at Risk of these portfolios.

The common approaches will be covered in the following sections. These approaches can also be applied to 'linear' portfolios, which would then take into account the effect of the very small non-linearities of those portfolios.

Regardless of the method of calculating the Value at Risk, it should always be compared against the Value at Risk Limit, as discussed in Chapter 7. It is also sensible to initiate a formal management discussion whenever the Value at Risk exceeds some nominated trigger level. Such a formal discussion should include a review of the conditions under which the maximum loss could occur, and should also make some estimate of the probability of occurrence of the particular set of market factors that would generate such a loss. If this probability is considered to be sufficiently low to make the chance of incurring the loss insignificant, then the position could be left open. In general, the open position is hedged as soon as is practicable. This trigger mechanism is one way of indicating that appropriate action has to be taken to ensure that the Value at Risk Limit is not exceeded.

8.2.1 Two Standard Deviation Changes in the Market Factor

The linear Value at Risk is often used as a first approximation to the Value at Risk in an option portfolio. It is calculated as shown earlier:

$$VAR = FS * (2\sigma)$$
$$= \text{Delta} * (2\sigma)$$

For option portfolios that have a low Gamma exposure, this is a reasonable approximation. However, for portfolios with significant Gamma exposure, this is a very poor approximation. In this case, a better estimate of the Value at Risk can be obtained by using both the Delta and the Gamma

$$VAR = \text{Delta} * (2\sigma) + 0.5 * \text{Gamma} * (2\sigma)^2$$

Because this is not symmetrical, the effect of an increase in the market factor is not equal and opposite to the effect of a decrease in the market factor. Different estimates of the Value at Risk can be derived for these two cases

$$VAR+ \; = \; 0.5 * \text{Gamma} * (2\sigma)^2 + \text{Delta} * (2\sigma)$$
$$VAR- \; = \; 0.5 * \text{Gamma} * (2\sigma)^2 - \text{Delta} * (2\sigma)$$

The actual Value at Risk is then taken to be whichever of these two values is the larger negative number. Both these estimates are calculated at the total portfolio level, using the Delta and Gamma that have already been calculated to assist with the regular management of the portfolio. In order to obtain any more accurate estimates, it is necessary to revalue all the transactions in the portfolio individually.

The simplest method is to value all the transactions in the portfolio using a market factor that has been changed by two standard deviations. To do this, the portfolio is valued using the current market rate; then it is valued using the current market rate increased by two standard deviations and then it is valued using the current market rate decreased by two standard deviations. This shows both the magnitude of the potential loss and the direction in which the market factor has to move to produce such a loss, if the change in value is indeed a loss. It is perfectly feasible for an option portfolio to show gains in both directions. If there are losses in both directions, it is usual to select the greater loss as the Value at Risk.

Unfortunately, with a large portfolio of options the worst case loss is not necessarily caused by a large movement in the underlying market factor. It is perfectly feasible for a one standard deviation move to cause a larger loss than a two standard deviation move. Consequently, this method of calculating the Value at Risk is usually performed by valuing the portfolio for a reasonable number of values of the underlying market factor. These values are at small intervals, perhaps one fifth of a standard deviation, out to two standard deviations in both directions. This gives a profit and loss profile of the portfolio for a range of changes in the underlying market factor. The Value at Risk is then taken to be the largest loss within the range of two standard deviations in the underlying market factor. For ease of reference, this informa-

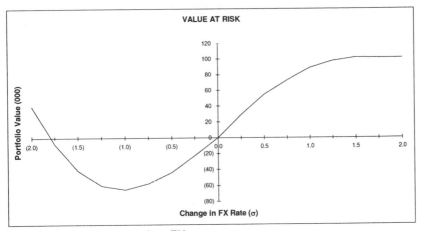

Figure 8.2 Valuation against FX rate

tion is often displayed graphically rather than as a set of numbers, and is an essential tool for the proper management of the portfolio.

In Figure 8.2, the Value at Risk is shown for a range of changes in the underlying market factor, namely a foreign exchange rate. It can be seen that the worst case loss of 65,000 does not occur at either a two standard deviation increase or a two standard deviation decrease, but rather at about a one standard deviation decrease in the foreign exchange rate. This refinement provides a much better estimate of the true Value at Risk.

The same approach can be taken for the other market factors. For example, in Figure 8.3, the value of the portfolio is shown for a range of values of volatility from minus two standard deviations to plus two standard deviations.

It can be seen that this is very roughly a linear relationship. The worst case loss of 73,000 occurs for a two standard deviation increase in volatility.

8.2.2 Multiple Market Factors

The approach outlined in the previous section resulted in a profit and loss profile for changes in a particular market factor. As there were two major market factors, this was done for the two market factors independently, and this does provide useful information

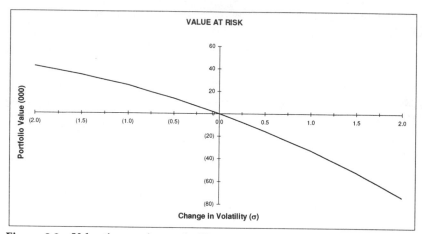

Figure 8.3   Valuation against volatility

for managing the portfolio. The two important market factors
determining the value of an option are the underlying instrument
and the volatility of the underlying instrument; the effect of interest rates is quite small in comparison. For example, in a DEM/
USD foreign exchange option, the spot DEM/USD foreign exchange rate is one important market factor – the underlying instrument – and the volatility of that foreign exchange rate is the
other important market factor – the volatility of the underlying
instrument. Changes in the interest rates in the two currencies
have a relatively minor effect.

Once the worst case losses for changes in the two major market factors have been established, they need to be combined in
some manner. It is not unusual to take the most conservative approach and simply add the two numbers. This gives a total of
65,000 + 73,000 = 138,000. Alternatively it could be assumed that
the two market factors are completely independent - a rather ag-
gressive assumption - and then the combined Value at Risk would
be the square root of the sum of the squares of the individual
Values at Risk, which gives a Value at Risk of 98,000. This is considerably lower than the figure of 138,000 derived under the conservative assumption.

Unfortunately, the mathematical complexity of option portfolios is such that the two market factors cannot be treated inde-

pendently. The effect of changes in the underlying instrument is different at different levels of volatility of that instrument, just as the effect of changes in the volatility of the underlying instrument is different at different levels of the underlying instrument.

To overcome this, the effect of changes in these two market factors should be examined simultaneously. This means that the profit and loss profile becomes a two-dimensional table instead of a simple set of numbers. If the results are displayed graphically, the result is a three-dimensional graph instead of a standard two-dimensional graph. For Value at Risk calculations, the range of this graph on both axes is from the current market rate minus two standard deviations to the current market rate plus two standard deviations. A typical graph for a foreign exchange option portfolio is shown in Figure 8.4.

This form of analysis will reveal the greatest loss within the range selected, whether that loss is at the minimum or the maximum of the range selected or whether it is at some intermediate or internal point. With a portfolio comprised of a number of standard options - bought and sold options, put and call options, all with different strike prices – an internal minimum is perfectly feasible. When a significant number of complex options are included, for example, barrier options an internal minimum becomes even more likely.

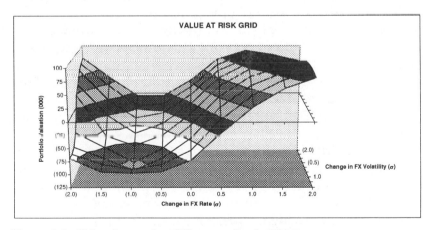

Figure 8.4   Valuation against FX rate and volatility

In the Figure 8.4, the minimum value of (112,000) occurs for approximately a one standard deviation decrease in the foreign exchange rate and a one standard deviation increase in the volatility of the foreign exchange rate. This minimum value can be regarded as a better estimate of the Value at Risk than the linear Value at Risk, as it is the worst case loss within two standard deviation changes in both market factors. This figure can be compared with (98,000) assuming independence of the two market factors and (138,000) assuming minus 100% correlation of the two market factors.

8.2.3 Back-testing Method

The **back-testing method** is sometimes referred to as a 'simulation method', in particular as the 'historical simulation' method. I have reserved the term 'simulation' for the Monte Carlo simulation method discussed in the next section. The essence of this method is as follows.

In order to use this method, a complete history of all the market factor data is required – typically, daily rates over a five-year period. The current portfolio of transactions is then valued using the market factor data of each trading day throughout the last five years. The daily profit or loss that would have arisen for each trading day over the last five years is recorded; this is simply the change in value of the portfolio from the value of the previous day. This will result in an array of 1,260 observations of the daily profit and loss. These figures are then sorted into an array in ascending order, so that the greatest loss is the first member of the array. The Value at Risk is then set equal to the 29th member of that array – the 97.7% confidence level for an array of 1,260 observations.

Because actual historical market data is used to value the portfolio, all the correlations that have existed between the various market factors are maintained by this method. The data will show, for example, that European foreign exchange rates against the US dollar maintain a high degree of correlation. Five years of history will also include the devaluation of certain European currencies against the other European currencies. It should be noted that a single devaluation will be ignored by this method, because a single devaluation will only affect one potential loss; with the Value at Risk set at the 97.7% confidence level, the 28 worst case losses are ignored when five years of historical data are used. However, the exchange rate of a currency usually exhibits higher volatility both before and after a devaluation, so some of this higher volatility will be reflected in the Value at Risk.

This method is often applied to foreign exchange portfolios, because the result is easy to interpret: if the current portfolio had been held on every day in the last five years, on only 29 of those days would the institution have suffered a loss greater than or equal to the given Value at Risk. As this is a non-parametric approach, the Value at Risk can easily be quoted at the 97.7% level (29 days) or the 99.9% level (1 day). The ability to give the results for a range of confidence levels is a very useful feature of this approach.

If the portfolio contains a reasonably large number of transactions, then, in order to value that portfolio of transactions on every trading day over the last five years, a very large number of transaction valuations will have to be performed. There are a number of methods that are employed to reduce the time that this process will take.

Firstly, the calculation can be done at portfolio position level. This is particularly applicable to foreign exchange portfolios, in which the entire portfolio of transactions is present valued at current market rates to produce the net open position in every currency, long or short. In effect, this method ignores interest rate risk in order to obtain a rapid calculation of the foreign exchange risk. Once the net open positions in each currency have been obtained, they are valued using the five years of historical foreign exchange rates to determine the 97.7% worst case daily loss – the Value at Risk. The effect of changing interest rates from one day to the next is completely ignored, as this is small in comparison with the effect of changing the foreign exchange rates. Because this method values the position in each currency instead of valuing each individual transaction, there will be a reduction in processing time of two or three orders of magnitude; in a portfolio of 10,000 transactions involving only 10 currencies, this method will run 1,000 faster.

The second method is to use the full factor sensitivity analysis of the portfolio, thereby utilizing a linear approximation. The daily change in the value of each particular market factor is ascertained, and multiplied by the factor sensitivity of the portfolio to changes in that market factor, thereby obtaining the change in the value of the portfolio due to changes in that market factor. This is then repeated for every market factor, and the effect of these individual changes are summed with sign to calculate the daily change in the value of the portfolio. These changes are then sorted to obtain the potential loss at the 97.7% confidence level – the Value at Risk. The simple summation in this method implicitly assumes that the various market factors are not correlated. The total change in value due to two market factors changing simultaneously is set to be the sum of the changes in value due to each market factor changing independently. This is a reasonable assumption for linear portfolios.

The third method is similar to the second, except that it uses a non-linear Taylor series expansion instead of the linear factor sensitivity analysis. Typically, this is only used for option portfolios in which both the Delta and the Gamma are already known, because they are calculated by the product system to assist the trader in managing the portfolio. However, conceptually there is no requirement to restrict the expansion to the first two terms, Delta and Gamma. Higher order terms could be used if the product systems were able to calculate them.

The fourth method takes into account the interaction between two different market factors, such as in an option portfolio where there is a strong interaction between two market factors: the underlying and the volatility of the underlying. This is done by using the two-dimensional grid discussed in the Section 8.2.2. In this method, the daily changes in the values of the two market factors are ascertained from the historical data. Thus to apply this method to an option portfolio, five years of daily history of implied volatility are required, and for many options this is not readily available. The resultant change in the value of the portfolio due to changes in these two market factors is obtained by interpolation in both directions in the grid of values. This interpolation is usually a linear interpolation, because the grid is usually sufficiently fine for this to be a good approximation. Again, higher order interpolation routines could be used if it was felt that this was justifiable. The resultant daily changes are then sorted to obtain the potential loss at the 97.7% confidence level – the Value at Risk.

The back-testing method has major shortcomings when used for option portfolios. This is best explained by using an example in which we will compare a forward foreign exchange transaction with a foreign exchange option. Let us assume that an institution whose base currency is US dollars enters into a forward foreign exchange contract to buy GBP 1,000,000 in exchange for USD 1,500,000 which is at a rate of 1.50 USD/GBP. We now calculate the change in the value of this contract for the same change in the foreign exchange rate, but from three different spot foreign exchange rates, namely 1.40, 1.50 and 1.60. The results are in Table 8.1.

For a forward foreign exchange contract, the level of the current spot rate does not affect the change in value of the contract - it is 10,000 in all three cases. However, the results are quite different for a foreign exchange option at a strike price of 1.50 with one month to maturity.

For a foreign exchange option contract, the level of the current spot rate has a significant effect on the change in value of the contract – it varies from 681 to 5,365 to 9,387 in the example shown in Table 8.2. Consequently, any attempt to use the back-testing

Table 8.1 Forward foreign exchange transaction

FX Rate	GBP Amount	In USD	USD Amount	Value	Change in Value
1.40	1,000,000	1,400,000	(1,500,000)	(100,000)	
1.41	1,000,000	1,410,000	(1,500,000)	(90,000)	10,000
1.50	1,000,000	1,500,000	(1,500,000)	0	
1.51	1,000,000	1,510,000	(1,500,000)	10,000	10,000
1.60	1,000,000	1,600,000	(1,500,000)	100,000	
1.61	1,000,000	1,610,000	(1,500,000)	110,000	10,000

Table 8.2 Foreign exchange option

FX Rate	Option Value	Change in Value
1.40	1,474	
1.41	2,155	681
1.50	25,785	
1.51	31,150	5,365
1.60	101,515	
1.61	110,902	9,387

method for options must address this problem. One possible solution would be to adjust the strike price of every option so that the adjusted strike price in the back-testing model bears the same ratio to the spot price in the model as the actual strike price does to the actual spot price. This does remove a major part of the problem, but it is still not an entirely satisfactory method.

In all cases, the methods are searching for the potential loss at the 97.7% confidence level over the five years of actual history. Because actual historical market data is used, this is a particularly straightforward concept that is relatively easy to understand. If the institution had held the current portfolio on every day during the last five years, on only 29 of those days would the institution have suffered a loss greater than or equal to the computed Value at Risk.

8.2.4 Simulation Techniques

Whereas the back-testing method uses actual historical market data to value the portfolio every day throughout the historical period, the **Monte Carlo simulation method** only uses the historical market data to calculate the variance/covariance matrix. This matrix was discussed in Chapter 6. It is a symmetric matrix which has the variances of every market factor down the diagonals and the covariances between the various market factors in the off-diagonal terms.

The Monte Carlo simulation process starts by valuing the entire portfolio of transactions using all the current market rates for each market factor. This gives the current mark-to-market value of the portfolio, which is the benchmark value against which the potential losses are measured.

The next step is to simulate one potential set of values for all the market factors on the following day. This is done by randomly selecting the change in each market factor from its normal distribution – a distribution whose width is given by the variance of the market factor as stored in the variance/covariance matrix. This is done for each market factor, so that a complete set of market factors is obtained for the following day.

Such a simplified approach ignores the problem of correlation between the various market factors, and so could result in two highly correlated market factors moving dramatically in opposite directions. To avoid this, the full variance/covariance matrix is used to supply information on these correlations. If a complete set of changes in the market factors is obtained by selecting randomly from the appropriate normal distributions, then this can be converted to a set of correlated changes by pre-multiplying the vector of changes by the square root of the variance/covariance matrix. The resultant vector of changes maintains the correlations between the changes in the various market factors. Full details of this procedure are given in any standard statistics textbook in the discussion of multivariate normal distributions.

These changes are then applied to the current market rates in order to obtain one complete set of market factors for the following day. This set is then used to value every transaction in the portfolio. This process is repeated 1,000 times, each with a different set of random numbers generated from the normal distributions of the individual market factors. These 1,000 different values of the portfolio are then sorted into sequential order, and the 23rd worst case is selected. This is the two standard deviation worst case potential change in the portfolio value over the next day – the 97.7% confidence level Value at Risk. One thousand simulations is a suitable number, as it represents a suitable compromise between the need for a reasonable level of statistical accuracy and the need for reduced computational times.

If the back-testing method described in the previous section uses five years of actual historic data, the worst case loss that would have happened on any day during the last five years can be determined. With 1,260 observations, statistically this is not a problem, because the 97.7% confidence level is the 29th observation. In general, there are only small differences between the 28th, the 29th and the 30th observations in a series of 1,260 observations. However, if significantly less history is available, such as a mere six months of data, the back-testing method runs into problems with its statistics as the 97.7% confidence level value is the third in the series. Because the distribution is only sparsely populated, there is usually quite a large difference between the second, third and fourth observations. The simulation procedure does not suffer from this disadvantage, as sufficient simulations can be run to ensure sufficient statistics are available, even when only six months of historical data are available. The only problem is then the validity of the variance/covariance matrix, when it is calculated from insufficient data.

As mentioned earlier, with a large portfolio of transactions, the valuation of each individual transaction under 1,000 different market factor scenarios can be a very computer-intensive calculation. All the methods that were used to reduce this problem in the back-testing method can also be used to reduce the problem here, so that the need to value the entire portfolio at least 1,000 times under the 1,000 different market factor scenarios does not place too great a demand on the computer resources of the institution.

There is no doubt that the Value at Risk calculation using matrix multiplication of factor sensitivities is the much faster method and is also sufficiently accurate for linear products. The Value at Risk calculation using Monte Carlo simulation is the much slower method, but is far more accurate for non-linear products.

CHAPTER NINE

Stress Testing

9.1 Stress Testing

The Value at Risk methodology outlined in previous chapters produces an estimate of the potential loss at a reasonably high level of confidence, such as the 97.7% confidence level of the amount that could be lost in one day. However, this is based on statistical estimates of the likely moves in the underlying market factors, and these statistical estimates are based on an analysis of the historical data for the underlying market factor. Such an analysis is particularly relevant to the normal day-to-day operation of an institution, as such potential losses will occur from time to time. When such a loss does occur, the institution must be able to absorb the loss against its revenue.

It is becoming increasingly important that the institution should also monitor the effects of much larger changes in these underlying market factors, such an overnight change equivalent to a 99% confidence level change over a two-week period. The effect of changes of this magnitude are also of interest to the banking regulators in many countries.

Under a normal distribution, such changes are an exceedingly unlikely occurrence. Therefore, when the effect of these much larger changes is examined, it is more appropriate to ensure that the institution has sufficient capital to cover the potential loss, rather than be expected to cover the loss out of revenue. As changes of this magnitude do indeed occur from time to time, the survival of the institution must not be at threat – it must have sufficient capital to absorb such a loss.

9.2 Stress Testing Using Worst Case Scenarios

Another method of tackling stress testing is to assume a particular set of circumstances that are possible, though extremely improbable, and to work through the ramifications of this set of assumptions. This is often a very time-consuming exercise that results in numbers that are of very little relevance to the institution. However, the effort of working through all these ramifications may reveal other problems that the institution should have tackled.

For example, one possible set of circumstances could include the immediate shut-down of one particular branch office in a particular market. If this resulted in the cessation of all trading for a month or more until an alternative operating site was found, the outcome could be an unacceptably high potential loss caused by running open positions for some considerable time until they were recognized and closed out. The temporary loss of customer revenue could be overshadowed by the permanent loss of some customers, who did not return when the institution was back in business. Therefore, such an analysis should not be confined to simply calculating the Value at Risk over a one month period, but should also examine these other consequences. The worst case could be regarded as such a significant threat to the survival of the institution that the existing back-up procedures should be significantly improved.

The real problem with this approach is that the improbable scenario is not necessarily a worst case. The scenario itself may be generally regarded as a worst case, but it is perfectly possible that the institution could be positioned to profit from such a scenario. Clearly, the effect of this improbable scenario will change as the positions of the institution change from day to day. Thus the numbers that are actually generated by such a scenario are not as useful as the exercise of producing them, which could identify other weaknesses in the management of risk in the institution.

The **stress test value** that is produced by such a worst case scenario analysis is usually compared to the capital of the institution simply to see whether the institution could actually survive such a set of conditions and still continue to operate. It is not a number to be compared to the monthly revenue of the institution, because it represents an extremely improbable, though still possible, case.

9.3 Stress Testing using the Value at Risk Methodology

Stress testing attempts to identify the losses that could occur in a given portfolio under possible, though highly improbable, changes in the market factors that govern the value of the particular portfolio. There are many forms of stress testing, and the common approaches will be covered in the following sections.

It is also useful to have a formal management discussion if the stress test value exceeds a nominated trigger level, such as a given multiple of the Value at Risk limit. In this case, such a formal discussion should include a review of the conditions under which the maximum loss could occur, and should also make some estimate of the probability of occurrence of the particular set of market factors that would generate such a loss. If this probability is considered to be sufficiently low that the chance of incurring the loss is insignificant, then the position could be left open. It is often the case in complex option portfolios that the conditions under which a large loss could occur are regarded as being extremely unlikely. For example, it is extremely unlikely that a large change in a foreign exchange rate would be accompanied by a large reduction in the volatility of that foreign exchange rate.

Although the Value at Risk limit is usually set in relation to expected revenue of the business unit, it is far more appropriate for the stress test limit to be set in relation to the capital that has been allocated to the business unit by the institution.

The simplest forms of stress testing are similar to the Value at Risk methods outlined in Chapter 8. The only difference is that the changes in the underlying market factors are much greater: the 97.7% confidence level one day Value at Risk is replaced by a 99% confidence level 10-day stress test value. Under the normal distribution assumption, this is equivalent to a 7.36 standard deviation daily move. In the interests of simplicity and conservatism, this will be rounded up to eight standard deviations in the following analysis.

9.3.1 Large Changes in the Market Factor

The linear Value at Risk can be used to derive a first approximation to the stress test value. It is calculated as shown earlier:

$$STV = FS * (8\sigma)$$

For option portfolios, a better estimate of the stress test value can be obtained by using both the Delta and the Gamma. Because the effect of an increase in the market factor is not equal and opposite to the effect of a decrease in the market factor, we derive two estimates for the stress test value and then take the larger negative value.

$$
\begin{aligned}
STV + &= 0.5 * \text{Gamma} * (8\sigma)^2 + \text{Delta} * (8\sigma) \\
STV - &= 0.5 * \text{Gamma} * (8\sigma)^2 - \text{Delta} * (8\sigma) \\
STV &= \text{Min}[STV+, STV-]
\end{aligned}
$$

Both these estimates are calculated at the total portfolio level, using the Delta and Gamma that have already been calculated to assist with the regular management of the portfolio. To obtain a better estimate, it is necessary to revalue all the individual transactions in the portfolio.

The simplest form of stress testing is to value the portfolio under the assumption that there will be a large eight standard deviation change in the value of the underlying market factor. The portfolio is valued using the current market rate, and then using the current market rate increased by eight standard deviations and then using the current market rate decreased by eight standard deviations. This gives two changes in value from the current valuation, and the stress test value is then set as the greater loss of the two changes in value.

For linear portfolios, this test consists of the simple step of multiplying the Value at Risk by four. For option portfolios, the test is performed as stated above.

As with the Value at Risk calculation, the worst case loss is not necessarily caused by a large movement in the underlying market factor. It is perfectly feasible for eight standard deviation moves to produce gains in both directions, rather than losses. It is perfectly feasible for a four standard deviation move to cause a larger loss than an eight standard deviation move. Consequently, this form of stress testing is usually performed by valuing the portfolio at intervals of one standard deviation out to eight standard deviations in both directions to obtain a profit and loss profile of the portfolio. The stress test value is then set to be the greatest loss shown in this profit and loss profile over the wide range of values of the underlying market factor. A sample graph is shown in Figure 9.1.

It can be seen that the maximum loss of 259,000 occurs at minus four standard deviations and not at the extremes of plus and minus eight standard deviations.

9.3.2 Multiple Market Factors

The approach outlined in the previous section resulted in a stress test value selected from the profit and loss profile for changes in a particular market factor. This can be done for two market fac-

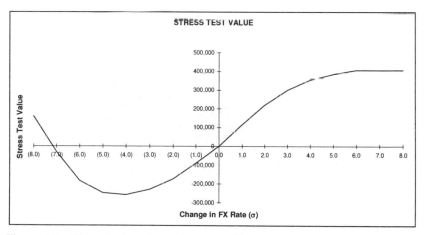

Figure 9.1   Stress test profit and loss profile

tors independently and the resultant values summed to provide a useful stress test value.

However, it is more appropriate to examine the effect of changes in the two major market factors simultaneously. The stress test value is then taken from the two-dimensional table of profit and loss numbers by choosing the greatest loss within the range selected, whether that loss is at the minimum or the maximum of the range selected or whether it is at some intermediate point. With a much wider range of market factors than is used for the calculation of Value at Risk, it is quite likely that the minimum will not be at the extremes of the range selected. This minimum value is the stress test value and is shown in Figure 9.2.

It can be seen that the maximum loss of 766,000 occurs when the foreign exchange rate decreases by six standard deviations and the volatility of the foreign exchange rate increases by eight standard deviations. This maximum loss is the stress test value.

9.3.3 Back-testing Method

The back-testing method for estimating the Value at Risk can be adapted to calculate the stress test value. The essence of this method is as follows.

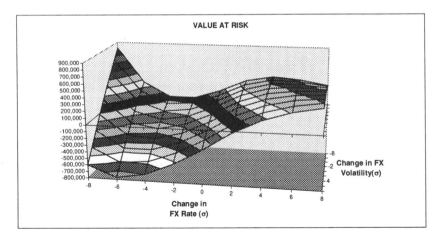

Figure 9.2   Stress test value

As with the Value at Risk method, a complete history of all the market factor data is required – typically daily rates over a five-year period – and the current portfolio of transactions is then valued using the market factor data of each trading day throughout the last five years. The profit or loss arising from holding the current portfolio for the 10 trading day period starting five years ago is recorded. The 10 trading day period starting one trading day later is then examined, and the profit or loss of that period is recorded. This is repeated for all 10 trading day periods during the last five years, which will result in an array of some 1,250 observations. These loss figures are then sorted into an array in ascending order, so that the greatest loss is the first member of the array. The stress test value is then set at the 99% confidence level, which will be either the 12th or the 13th member of the array, depending upon whether an extra conservative bias is required or not.

It must be stressed that this assumes that the portfolio is held for the entire period, even though it contains spot transactions that would normally settle well before the 10-day period is over. This is particularly important for options that are approaching maturity, because otherwise the diminishing time to maturity would result in rapidly changing option values. The time to maturity is held constant throughout the 10-day period. As in the Value at Risk calculation, option strike prices have to be adjusted so that the ratio of the exercise price to the spot price at the start of each 10-day period is identical to the current ratio of exercise price to spot price.

One minor variant of the above method is that instead of recording the change in value from the beginning to the end of the 10-day period, the greatest loss on any day during the 10-day period is recorded. If the value of the portfolio depends upon certain market factors that infrequently exhibit one large swing followed by an immediate recovery, this variant will give a larger stress test value than the straightforward method, because the one bad day will contribute to 10 observations rather than one observation. If there has only been one large swing in the five years of history, the distinction is not particularly relevant, as it will be ignored by selecting the 99% confidence level.

As with the Value at Risk calculation, the use of actual historical market data means that all the correlations that exist between
the various market factors are maintained. Five years of history
will also include the devaluation of certain European currencies
against the other European currencies. Although the stress test is
run at a much higher confidence level than Value at Risk, a single
devaluation will still be ignored by this method, because a single
devaluation will only affect 10 potential losses. The stress test
value is a 99% confidence level, so the 13 worst case losses are
ignored when five years of historical data are used. However, the
exchange rate of a currency usually exhibits higher volatility both
before and after a devaluation, so this higher volatility will un-
doubtedly be reflected in the stress test value.

In order to avoid the valuation of the entire portfolio of transactions on every trading day over the last five years, the methods
used to avoid this time-consuming process in Value at Risk calculations can also be used in stress test value calculations. In each
of these methods, the stress test value can be calculated using
either of the two variants: these are the actual change over the 10-
day period and/or the greatest loss during the 10-day period.

Firstly, the calculation can be done at portfolio position level.
This is particularly applicable to foreign exchange portfolios, in
which the entire portfolio of transactions is present valued at current market rates to produce the net open position in every currency, long or short. Once the net open positions have been obtained, they are valued using the five years of historical foreign
exchange rates to determine the 99% worst case loss over any 10
trading day period – the stress test value. The effect of changing
interest rates over the 10-day period is ignored in the pursuit of
rapid computation.

The second method is to use the full factor sensitivity analysis
of the portfolio, thereby utilizing a linear approximation. The
change in the value of each particular market factor over the 10
trading day period is ascertained and multiplied by the factor
sensitivity of the portfolio to changes in that market factor, thereby
obtaining the change in the value of the portfolio due to changes
in that market factor. These individual changes are then summed
with sign to calculate the change in the value of the portfolio over

the 10 trading day period. These changes are then sorted to obtain the potential loss at the 99% confidence level – the stress test value.

The third method is similar to the second, except that it uses a non-linear Taylor series expansion instead of the linear factor sensitivity analysis. Typically, this is only used for option portfolios in which both the Delta and the Gamma are already known. Higher order terms could be used if the product systems were able to calculate them.

The fourth method takes into account the interaction between two different market factors, such as in an option portfolio. In this method, the changes in the values of the two market factors over the 10 trading day period are ascertained and the resultant change in the value of the portfolio due to changes in these two market factors is obtained by linear interpolation in both directions in the two-dimensional grid of profit and loss values. Other interpolation methods could be used, but the grid is usually sufficiently fine for linear interpolation to be a good approximation. The resultant changes for every 10-day period are then sorted to obtain the potential loss at the 99% confidence level – the stress test value.

In all cases, the methods are searching for the potential loss during 10-day periods at the 99% confidence level over the five years of actual history. Because actual historical market data is used, this is a particularly straightforward concept that is relatively easy to understand. If the institution had held the current portfolio on every day during the last five years, on only 13 of those days would the institution have suffered a loss of more than the stress test value over the following 10 days.

9.3.4 Simulation Techniques

The Monte Carlo simulation process discussed under the calculation of Value at Risk can also be used to calculate a stress test value.

This starts by valuing the entire portfolio of transactions using all the current market rates for each market factor. This gives the current mark-to-market value of the portfolio, which is the benchmark value against which the potential losses are measured. The next step is to simulate one potential set of values for all the market factors on the following day. This is done by randomly selecting the change in each market factor from its normal distribution, using the variance/covariance matrix so that all correlations are maintained. These changes are then applied to the current market rates in order to obtain a complete set of market factors for the following day, which is then used to value the entire set of transactions.

Having simulated the first day ahead, the next step is to simulate a potential set of values of all the market factors for the second day ahead, starting with the market factors of the first day ahead. This is done in the same manner as the first step. This set of market factors is then used to value the entire set of transactions. Usually 10 daily steps are taken, as this is regarded as a sufficiently long period to produce reasonably large changes in the market factors. The final change in the value of the portfolio is noted.

The entire process is then repeated 1,000 times, each with a different set of random numbers generated from the normal distributions of the individual market factors. These 1,000 different values of the portfolio are then sorted into sequential order, and the 10th worst case is selected. This is the 99% confidence level of the worst case potential change in the portfolio value over the next 10 days – the stress test value. Again, 1,000 simulations is an appropriate number, as it represents a suitable compromise between the need for statistical accuracy and the need for reduced computational times.

In order to produce the 10-day 99% confidence level stress test value, the terms and conditions of every contract are held constant throughout the period. This means that the time to maturity of every contract is also held constant – no transactions mature during the 10-day period, including spot transactions.

As mentioned earlier, with a large portfolio of transactions, the valuation of each individual transaction under 1,000 different market factor scenarios can be a very computer-intensive calculation. All the methods that were described earlier to avoid this problem are even more important in a simulation run. This is because of the need to value the entire portfolio every day at least 10,000 times under the 1,000 thousand different market factor scenarios.

An alternative approach to stress testing can be run using a variant of the Monte Carlo simulation process described above. Instead of assuming that all the transactions are held throughout the 10-day period, they are deleted from the portfolio when they reach their maturity dates. The worst case loss during the period is then estimated at the 97.7% confidence level. This approach is not seeking to find the effect of one large move in all market factors, but is looking at the effect over a 10-day period of not closing any new business, but simply allowing the existing portfolio to run off. In addition, no adjustments to any hedge are allowed during the 10-day period. In this case, the calculation cannot be run at the total portfolio level; every transaction has to be valued every day. This method is a form of scenario analysis, in that it estimates the impact under normal market conditions (97.7% confidence level) of ceasing to trade in a given location.

The stress test value calculation using matrix multiplication of factor sensitivities is fast and accurate for linear products. However, when the portfolio includes non-linear products, the stress test value calculation using Monte Carlo simulation becomes the only suitable method.

CHAPTER TEN

Capital Requirements

10.1 Economic Capital for Market Risk

No treatment of the subject of market risk would be complete without some discussion as to the level of economic capital required to cover the market risks that an institution undertakes. Before it is possible to decide exactly what the level of economic capital should be, it is necessary to define the reasons for holding that economic capital in the first place.

There are two alternative reasons for holding economic capital. The first is to cover the potential 'trading losses' of the institution at some appropriately high level of confidence, where the term trading loss is understood to mean the total losses in the trading businesses as a whole. The second is to cover the variability of the profit and loss in the trading businesses.

This presents each institution with an important choice, especially where part of the revenue stream is of a steady nature – for example, customer spread revenue or accrual revenue – and another part of the revenue stream is due to the taking of market risk, such as positioning or laying off customer transactions in the inter-bank market. In such a case, the fundamental question is whether the steady stream revenue should act as a buffer for the more variable risk-taking revenue.

Let us take, as an example, an institution in which the steady stream revenue is greater than the high-confidence-level potential losses from market risk. If the purpose is to guard against an overall loss, then no economic capital at all is required. However, if the purpose is to guard against the variability of the profit and loss of the institution, then economic capital would be required. Of course, the two alternatives only differ in the level of the steady stream revenue.

The standard approach to economic capital is simply based on the Value at Risk number. The Value at Risk represents the potential loss over a one-day period at the 97.7% confidence level. Thus the economic capital to be associated with this market risk should be some simple multiple of this Value at Risk. Different institutions use very different multipliers, ranging from as low as one to as high as 16. The latter number essentially annualizes the daily potential loss by scaling it by the square root of the number of trading days in a year. Since economic capital is usually assigned for a full year period, there is a great deal of logic behind the choice of this apparently high multiplier.

For many financial institutions, the amount of economic capital required to cover their market risk exposures is relatively low compared to the amount of capital required to back their credit risk exposures. Consequently, the actual level of the multiplier is not really a serious problem. It is far more important to ensure that the Value at Risk number is correctly calculated, since an inaccurate or approximate calculation can easily be in error by several orders of magnitude.

This means that proper attention must be paid to a number of points. Many of these relate to the construction of the variance/covariance matrix, since this is used in both the matrix multiplication method and the simulation method for calculating Value at Risk.

- The factor sensitivities of all future cash flows must be accurately assigned to the points on the maturity grid of the appropriate yield curve, using the correct zero coupon discount factor methodology.
- The variance/covariance matrix must contain the covariances between all the points on the maturity grid of each yield curve.
- The variance/covariance matrix must contain the covariances between all the points on the maturity grid of a given yield curve and all the points on the maturity grid of each other yield curve in that currency.
- The variance/covariance matrix must contain the covariances between all the points on the maturity grid of all the yield curves in a given currency and all the points on the maturity grid of

all the yield curves in every other currency.

- Similarly, in addition to the covariances between all interest rates in all currencies, the variance/covariance matrix must contain the covariances between all foreign exchange rates, between all equity prices, between the volatilities of all interest rates, between the volatilities of all foreign exchange rates, between the volatilities of all equity prices, and so on. These are the market factor groups.

- The variance/covariance matrix for interest rate volatilities is similar to the matrix for interest rates, in that there is a volatility curve corresponding to the yield curve. The variance/covariance matrix must contain the covariances between all the points on the maturity grid of all the volatility curves in a given currency and all the points on the maturity grid of all the volatility curves in every other currency.

- However, the variance/covariance matrix does not necessarily contain the covariances between market factors where those market factors fall into different market factor groups. Many of the correlations between market factors in different groups are in practice fairly low. For example, it is highly unlikely that there is any correlation between the volatility of a Southeast Asian equity index and the foreign exchange rate of a Latin American country. Thus it is a reasonable approximation to set these correlations and the corresponding covariances to zero.

- If the correlations between market factor groups are set to zero, then the Value at Risk can be calculated independently for each market factor group by the matrix multiplication method. This will be the best estimate of the Value at Risk arising from the entire group of market factors. The total Value at Risk is then the square root of the sum of the squares of the Value at Risk numbers for the different market factor groups.

- If the correlations between market factor groups are not set to zero, then one huge matrix multiplication will directly give the total Value at Risk. With zero correlations between the market factor groups, this method gives an identical result to the method in the previous point.

- If a much more conservative number is required, then the Value at Risk numbers for each of the market factor groups are simply added. This implies that the groups are either 100% correlated or minus 100% correlated, whichever gives the worst case.

• Finally, the aggregate Value at Risk is scaled up by 16, or by whatever scaling factor the institution has decided to implement, to obtain the required economic capital.

As the above methodology is only accurate for estimating the Value at Risk from linear instruments, some institutions prefer to use a methodology that takes into account the effect of non-linearity in option portfolios, such as one based on the Monte Carlo simulation of the entire portfolio. If this methodology is used, then the variance/ covariance matrix is needed to simulate the multivariate normal distributions of all the market factors. In this case, all the above points describing the contents of the matrix will still apply. This and other methodologies were discussed in Chapter 8.

Regardless of the particular technique that is used to calculate the Value at Risk, the economic capital requirement is obtained by multiplying by the Value at Risk by a scaling factor, such as 16.

The economic capital allocated to a business unit distils into a single number the risk of the business unit. Thus it can be used to estimate the return on risk of the business unit. To do this properly, the total economic capital is needed, especially the capital required to cover credit risk. These other forms of economic capital are not within the scope of this book.

10.2 Regulatory Capital for Market Risk

The need to estimate capital requirements comes not only from the need to assign the capital of the institution among the various risk-taking units to measure their return on capital, but also from the various regulatory bodies that require financial institutions to have sufficient capital to cover their risks. There are two major components to regulatory capital – capital to cover market risk and capital to cover credit risk. However, not only is regulatory capital for market risk measured differently to the economic capital of an institution, but there are also conflicting capital requirements within the regulatory community.

There are two major documents covering capital requirements for market risk. In April 1995, the Basle Committee on Banking Supervision, under the auspices of the Bank for International Settlements, issued a paper entitled 'Planned Supplement to the Capital Accord to Incorporate Market Risks' With a few minor changes, this proposal was confirmed in December 1995 and issued in January 1996 as 'Amendment to the Capital Accord to Incorporate Market Risks'. In April 1995, the Bank of England also issued a notice to institutions authorized under the Banking Act entitled 'Implementation in the United Kingdom of the Capital Adequacy Directive'. A subsequent notice containing clarifications and minor amendments was issued in December 1995. These documents will be referred to hereafter as the 'BIS proposal' and the 'CAD document'.

The object of this chapter is to summarize the standard treatment of market risk in these two documents, and to show how the methods outlined in this book can be used within the standard treatments, including the use of internal Value at Risk models. Only those sections of the documents considered relevant will be discussed, and, as many minor points have been omitted to simplify the discussion, even that discussion must not be regarded as definitive. For complete details of the regulatory capital requirements, the reader is referred to the original documents referenced above.

10.3 Standard Method

10.3.1 Interest Rate Risk

There are two separate capital charges for interest rate-dependent instruments, one applying to the specific risk of each security and the other to the general market risk of the entire portfolio. The specific risk requirements are intended to cover the fact that individual securities can move against the general market. The specific risk capital charge is set as a percentage of the principal of the debt security, or the notional principal in the case of debt derivatives. These are summarized in the Table 10.1.

There is no equivalent to a specific risk charge in the Value at

Table 10.1 Specific risk requirements for debt securities

Debt Security	Specific Risk Capital %
Government Debt	0.00
Qualifying debt < 6 months	0.25
Qualifying debt 6–24 months	1.00
Qualifying debt >24 months	1.60
Non-qualifying debt	8.00

Risk methodology outlined in this book. It is possible to take such risks into account by defining market factors at a micro-level, but this approach would mean that the market factors would become specific risk factors and so lose most of their applicability – an approach that is not recommended. The best approach to handling such risk is in the calculation of capital to cover credit risk, where not only the possibility of default is considered but also the probability of credit migration and any other factors that could affect the credit spread of an issuer. Such credit spread reflects directly on price movements that are independent of general market movements.

Although the general market risk requirements have been developed in terms of conventional debt securities, they are intended to cover the interest rate risk of the entire portfolio. Interest rate derivatives can be converted into positions in the relevant underlying instruments, and then treated identically to conventional debt securities. For example, an interest rate swap is converted into two notional positions in government securities with the appropriate maturities – the fixed leg will have a maturity equivalent to the residual life of the swap, whereas the floating leg will have a maturity equivalent to the period until the next interest rate fixing date.

There is a choice between two principal methods of measuring the capital to cover the general market risk to interest rates, namely the **maturity method** and the **duration method**. Although the maturity method is somewhat simpler than the duration method, it generally produces the higher capital requirement of the two methods. Consequently, we will focus attention on the duration method.

Table 10.2   Time bands, time zones and yield changes

Tenor	BIS Change in Yield (Basis Points)	CAD Change in Yield (Basis Points)
Zone 1		
Less than 1 month	100	100
1 to 3 months	100	100
3 to 6 months	100	100
6 to 12 months	100	100
Zone 2		
1.0 to 1.9 years	90	85
1.9 to 2.8 years	80	85
2.8 to 3.6 years	75	85
Zone 3		
3.6 to 4.3 years	75	70
4.3 to 5.7 years	70	70
5.7 to 7.3 years	65	70
7.3 to 9.3 years	60	70
9.3 to 10.6 years	60	70
10.6 to 12 years	60	70
12 to 20 years	60	70
Over 20 years	60	70

The duration method consists of the following steps.

(a)   The price sensitivity of each instrument to a change in interest rates of between 60 and 100 basis points, depending upon the maturity of the instrument, is ascertained. The BIS proposal does not state exactly how the price sensitivity is to be calculated. The CAD document defines it as the modified duration of the instrument multiplied by the relevant change in interest rates as given in Table 10.2. In the terminology used in this book, the modified duration is analogous to the factor sensitivity of each individual instrument.

For OECD currencies, these interest rate movements cover a range of 6 to 16 daily standard deviations. For comparison purposes, a 99% confidence level 10-day change corresponds to 7.36 daily standard deviations.

(b)   The resulting sensitivity measures are then placed in a duration-based ladder containing the 15 time bands in the Table 10.2.

Table 10.3 Disallowance factors

ZONES	BIS	CAD
Within band	5	0
Within zone		
Zone 1	40	2
Zone 2	30	2
Zone 3	30	2
Between zones		
Zones 1 & 2	40	40
Zones 2 & 3	40	40
Zones 1 & 3	100	150

(c) The long and the short positions in each time band are then subjected to a vertical disallowance factor. This is done by taking the smaller of the long and the short positions – the matched position – and multiplying it by the vertical disallowance factor, which is given in Table 10.3. The reason underlying this vertical disallowance is that a cash flow at one end of a time band is not exactly matched by an opposite cash flow at the other end of the time band. This is certainly true when it is the cash flows themselves that are considered. However, when the modified durations (the factor sensitivities) are correctly allocated to the relevant points on the maturity grid, this can be a very good approximation indeed.

(d) The net position in each time band – the unmatched position – is obtained by subtracting the short positions from the long positions to obtain a net long or short position. The net positions in each time band are subjected to horizontal disallowances, firstly between the time bands within a zone, and then between the various zones. As in the case of vertical disallowances, the horizontal disallowances are applied to the matched positions across time bands and across time zones.

Obviously many of the parameters are different in the two regulatory approaches. It is to be hoped that these differences will be resolved before the proposals actually become requirements. The implementation date for the CAD was 1 January 1996, whereas the implementation date for the BIS proposal is two years later.

The above calculations are to be run for each individual currency and the aggregate capital requirement is then the sum of the capital requirements for each individual currency. This implies that the correlation between interest rates in different currencies is either plus 100% or minus 100%, whichever gives the larger capital requirement. This is far more conservative than the method for calculating economic capital outlined in Section 10.1, because it does not take into account any correlation between currencies.

The BIS document permits an alternative approach for institutions with large swap books. In essence, this approach takes the entire portfolio of swaps in a given currency and defines an equivalent portfolio, which is a portfolio containing a very small number of swaps, but which has exactly the same sensitivity to changes in interest rates as the entire original portfolio. This means that the factor sensitivities must be identical at every point down the yield curve.

Using factor sensitivity analysis, this equivalent portfolio can be found very easily. At each point on the maturity grid, it will be the single on-market bond which has exactly the same factor sensitivity to the interest rate at that point on the yield curve as does the entire swap portfolio. An on-market bond with a tenor equal to a point on the maturity grid only has non-zero factor sensitivity in the one tenor that corresponds to its final maturity. This means that the principal of the equivalent bond is easy to calculate once the factor sensitivity of the on-market bond has been established. However, it is the factor sensitivity itself that is required as input to the duration method, rather than the principal of the bond. There will be up to 16 bonds in the equivalent portfolio, and the general market risk of these 16 bonds is then calculated using the duration method as if they were the only bonds in the portfolio.

Clearly there is no reason to restrict such an approach to swap books. It is an equally valid approach for books of forward rate agreements, interest rate futures, and similar instruments. In fact, it is valid for all forms of interest rate risk, including the interest rate risk in foreign exchange and equity transactions.

The CAD document permits an alternative approach in which approval can be granted to use risk aggregation models, such as interest rate sensitivity models. The factor sensitivity approach outlined in this book is such a model. Because the interest rate factor sensitivity of a book at each point on the maturity grid is a measure of the modified duration of the book at that point on the grid, the factor sensitivities of the book can be taken straight into the duration method described above. This should produce a very sensible measure of the capital needed to cover the general market risk of a large book of interest rate dependent instruments.

Unfortunately, the CAD document does not allow non-amortizing bonds to be included in any risk aggregation model. They have to be treated using the standard method. This is a major shortcoming of the approach, which means that the method results in a very inaccurate measure of the capital requirement. As discussed in previous chapters, portfolios of swaps and forward rate agreements are often hedged with government bonds to eliminate the vast majority of the interest rate risk. Therefore, in a well-hedged portfolio, the interest rate risk of the government bonds has the opposite sign to the interest rate risk of the derivatives. If the derivatives are included in the risk aggregation model and the government bonds are excluded, then the resultant capital requirement will be considerably higher than it should be. This is because both the derivatives and the government bonds will give a positive capital requirement, even though their exposure to interest rate risk is in opposite directions.

Despite this major shortcoming, it is nevertheless extremely useful to aggregate the interest rate risk from thousands of swaps, forward rate agreements, foreign exchange transactions, equity transactions and options down to a dozen or so instruments.

The risk aggregation models can also be used to aggregate the Delta risk implicit in interest rate options, such as caps and floors and swaptions. This will be discussed in more detail in Section 10.3.4.

Before approval can be granted to use risk aggregation models, the institution must meet the minimum requirements of the BIS proposal for internal models, as set out in Section 10.5.

Both documents also permit the use of internal Value at Risk

models, which can include the effects of all the correlations between all the interest rates in all the currencies. Such internal
models can overcome some of the limitations discussed above,
but there are other problems with their use which will be covered
in Section 10.5.

10.3.2 Foreign Exchange Risk

The calculation of the capital requirements for the general market risk in foreign exchange is relatively straightforward in comparison to the complex methods needed for interest rate risk. There
is no specific risk requirement in foreign exchange trading, as
there is no equivalent to the single issuer of a debt security.

First of all, the net open position in each currency is calculated,
including the net Delta (or Delta-based) equivalent of foreign
exchange options. In essence, this is the factor sensitivity of the
total book to each foreign exchange rate scaled up by a factor of
100. The scaling factor is necessary because the factor sensitivity
to foreign exchange rates is the change in value for a one per cent
appreciation of the foreign currency.

The standard method calculates the sum of the net long positions and the sum of the net short positions and takes the greater of
these as the overall net open position. The capital charge is then 8%
of the net open position. The use of the net open position in this
method is roughly equivalent to assuming that all foreign exchange
rates have correlations of 50%, which is a fairly conservative average for the range of currencies of a typical institution.

For the foreign exchange book of a typical institution, this 8%
change in foreign exchange rates lies in the range of 6 to 16 daily
standard deviations, depending upon the currency pair. The 99%
confidence level 10-day change corresponds to 7.36 daily standard deviations.

However, the CAD document specifically states that approval
can be obtained for the back-testing model to calculate the capital requirement for foreign exchange risks. This model is identical to the back-testing model described in Chapter 8. The advantage of such a model is that it takes into account all the historical
correlations between foreign exchange rates, and yet is still rela-

tively easy to implement. However, the CAD document sets the capital requirement to 95% of the losses over any 10-day period in the last five years, or 99% of the losses over any 10-day period in the last three years, with a minimum of 2% of the net open position.

Both documents also permit the use of internal Value at Risk models, which can include the effects of all the correlations between all the foreign exchange rates. Such internal models can overcome some of the limitations discussed above, but there are other problems with their use which will be covered in Section 10.5.

10.3.3 Equity Risk

The calculation of the capital requirements for the general market risk of equities is even more straightforward than the calculation of general market risk for foreign exchange. However, the capital requirement for specific risk is somewhat more complicated.

Specific risk is calculated on the gross positions of the institution – the sum of the long and short positions regardless of sign – whereas general market risk is calculated on the net position of the institution – the sum of the long and short positions inclusive of sign.

There is a specific risk requirement of 8% for an individual equity under the BIS proposal, but this is reduced to 4% in the CAD document for equities that are listed in one of the qualifying countries, where the list of qualifying countries is essentially a list of OECD countries.

Under the BIS proposal there is a reduced specific risk requirement of 4% for a portfolio of equities that is liquid and well-diversified, with a further reduction to 2% for a position in an index that comprises a diversified portfolio of equities. A consequence of this is that 2% capital is required to cover the possibility, for example, that the FTSE index will move against the London equity market. The CAD avoids this consequence by reducing the specific risk charge to zero for approved equity indices.The specific risk requirements are summarized in the Table 10.4.

Table 10.4   Specific risk for equity instruments

Equity position	BIS	CAD	
		Non-qualifying countries	Qualifying countries
Individual equities	8 %	8 %	4 %
Liquid well-diversified	4 %		2 %
Equity indices	2 %		0 %

In order to calculate the capital requirements for general market risk, the net open position in each equity is calculated, including the net Delta (or Delta-based) equivalent of each equity option. In essence, this is the factor sensitivity of the total book to each equity scaled up by a factor of 100. The scaling factor is necessary because the factor sensitivity to equity prices is the change in value for a one per cent appreciation of the equity. Similar positions are also calculated for equity indices.

The capital charge for general market risk is 8% of the net open position of each equity and each equity index, regardless of whether the net open position is long or short. This movement corresponds to a daily change in the range of 5 to 10 standard deviations, depending upon the particular equity market. The 99% confidence level 10-day change corresponds to a daily change of 7.36 standard deviations. These individual capital charges are then added across all equities and equity indices. This method completely ignores the correlations between different equity markets and is equivalent to assuming either plus 100% or minus 100% correlation, whichever gives the larger number.

Both documents also permit the use of internal Value at Risk models, which can include the effects of all the correlations between all equities. Such internal models can overcome some of the limitations discussed above, but there are other problems with their use which will be covered in Section 10.5.

10.3.4 Option Risk

The treatment of the risk in options can be tackled in several different ways, depending upon the size of the option portfolio and the sophistication of the institution.

(a) Simplified approach
The BIS proposal contains a simplified approach, which is not intended for institutions with substantial options portfolios. The CAD document contains a simplified approach called the 'carve-out method'. Both of these are mathematically fairly simple, but descriptively rather complex. Thus they will not be discussed here. The interested reader is referred to the original documents.

(b) Delta-plus Method / Buffer Approach
This is an intermediate approach which is very similar to the linear approach outlined in this book. The description that follows is based on the BIS proposal, but the CAD document allows for the approval of option models, such as the one described here, but in which some of the numbers are likely to be different.

The Delta equivalent of the option is treated as if it were a cash position in the underlying. In this manner, the linear component of the interest rate risk, the foreign exchange risk or the equity risk of the underlying is incorporated into the standard method. However, there is an additional capital requirement to cover the non-linearity of the option – the Gamma risk.

The Gamma risk is calculated using the Taylor series expansion already discussed. For interest rate options, the net negative Gammas in each time band are multiplied by the risk weight in Table 10.5 and by the square of the market value of the underlying. For foreign exchange options, the net negative Gammas for each currency pair are multiplied by 0.32% and by the square of the market value of the position. For options on equities and equity indices, the net negative Gammas for each equity are multiplied by 0.32% and by the square of the market value of the position. For options on commodities, the net negative Gammas for each commodity are multiplied by 1.125% and by the square of the market value of the underlying. In all cases, every subset with a positive Gamma is simply ignored; they cannot be used to off-

Table 10.5 Risk weights for Gamma by time band

Time band	Modified duration (Assumed average)	Assumed change in interest rate (bpts)	Risk weight for Gamma (%)
Up to 1 month	0.00	100	0.00000
1 to 3 months	0.20	100	0.00020
3 to 6 months	0.40	100	0.00080
6 to 12 months	0.70	100	0.00245
1 to 2 years	1.25	90	0.00703
2 to 3 years	1.75	80	0.01225
3 to 4 years	2.25	75	0.01898
4 to 5 years	2.75	75	0.02836
5 to 7 years	3.25	70	0.03697
7 to 10 years	3.75	65	0.04570
10 to 15 years	4.50	60	0.06075
15 to 20 years	5.25	60	0.08269
Over 20 years	6.00	60	0.10800

set negative Gammas elsewhere. For interest rate options, the subsets are the different time bands in each currency. For foreign exchange options, the subsets are the different currency pairs. For equity options, the subsets are the different equities and equity indices.

This method requires capital to cover the possibility of greater losses than would be suggested from an analysis of the linear Delta by incorporating quadratic terms with negative Gamma and ignoring quadratic terms with positive Gamma. Thus it is a very conservative measure of the Gamma risk.

Capital requirements to cover the volatility risk are conceptually fairly straightforward. For all types of option, the Vega (factor sensitivity to volatility) is calculated for the appropriate subset of options and then a proportional change in volatility of 25% is imposed and the resultant change in value determined for each subset. For example, if the current implied volatility is 16%, then the Vega risk is the more negative of the changes in value given by a 12% volatility and a 20% volatility. The capital requirement is then the absolute value of the sum of the individual capital requirements for Vega risk for each subset.

(c) Scenario Analysis / Scenario Matrix Approach
The BIS proposal defines a scenario analysis method and the CAD document describes a scenario matrix approach. Both of these

are essentially the same as the stress test approach outlined in an Chapter 9. The change in value of the portfolio is produced in a two-dimensional matrix, in which the changes in value are calculated for changes in the underlying rate or price on one axis and changes in the volatility of the underlying rate or price along the other axis.

The ranges on each axis have been set as follows. For interest rates, the range is the highest assumed change for any time band within the zone, namely 100 basis points for zone 1, 90 basis points for zone 2 and 75 basis points for zone 3. The range for foreign exchange would be plus and minus 8%, and the range for equities would be plus and minus 12 %. For the volatility axis, the range would be a proportional change of plus and minus 25% of the current level of volatility.

The capital requirement for each subset of the total portfolio is the worst case loss anywhere within the scenario matrix. The total capital requirement is the sum of these worst case losses in portfolio value for each subset of the underlying rate or price. Separate calculations are required for each of the three zones in each currency, for each foreign exchange pair and for every underlying equity or equity index.

(d) Internal Models

Again, the regulatory bodies have the ability to approve the internal models of an institution for the calculation of capital requirements. Clearly the scenario matrix approach cannot be taken unless the institution already has an approved option model in place.

However, there is the possibility that other option models could be approved, which calculate Value at Risk taking into account the correlations within the major market factor groups.

10.4 Use of Factor Sensitivities with the Standard Method

The result of using the various methods described above is best illustrated with a sample portfolio of cash flows, whose general

Table 10.6 Sample portfolio

Month	Rate	Inflow	Outflow
1	5.5%	1100	1000
3	5.6%	2050	2000
6	5.8%	2000	2250
12	6.0%	2030	2000
24	6.2%	1015	1000
36	6.4%	1000	1025
48	6.6%	1020	1000
60	6.8%	500	520
72	6.9%	520	500
84	7.0%	510	500
96	7.1%	230	200
108	7.2%	200	220
120	7.3%	100	110
Total		12,275	12,325

market risk depends upon interest rates only. In this portfolio, all the cash inflows and the cash outflows fall exactly at the points on the maturity grid. This removes the problem of matching and also simplifies the calculation of an equivalent portfolio. However, it does mean that most of the capital requirements that would be generated by the vertical disallowances have already been eliminated, so this is not a typical portfolio. The sample portfolio is given in Table 10.6.

The capital requirement for this portfolio is shown in the Table 10.7 using five different methods to calculate the capital charge.

It can be seen that the maturity method gives extremely high capital requirements when compared to the duration method and the other methods, which is the reason that it has not been covered in this chapter. The duration method is considerably better under the CAD implementation proposals than under the BIS proposals, because the disallowance factors under the CAD are much smaller than under the BIS.

However, the **equivalent portfolio method** shows an even greater reduction in the capital requirement. This method effectively reduces all the cash flows at each maturity to a single bond,

Table 10.7   Capital requirement

	BIS	CAD
Maturity method	12.994	13.200
Duration method	8.289	3.932
Equivalent portfolio	1.605	1.082
Correlated VAR	0.132	0.132
Net VAR	0.016	0.016

and so the vertical disallowance factor essentially becomes zero.

The **correlated VAR method** is the one described in Section 7.2. The two standard deviation Value at Risk (one-day 97.7% confidence level) is calculated and then scaled up to a 10 day 99% confidence level.

The **net VAR** has not been described earlier. It is obtained by calculating the signed factor sensitivities at each point down the yield curve and then adding them to obtain the effect of a one basis point parallel shift in interest rates. This parallel shift factor sensitivity is then multiplied by the volatility of the one-year interest rate, as a proxy for the volatility of the entire yield curve. This is a quick method of obtaining a very approximate Value at Risk, but as it assumes that all yield curve movements are parallel shifts, it is not a method that can be seriously advocated.

10.5 Use of Internal Models

The BIS proposal for market risk allows the use of internal models to meet the regulatory capital requirements, but these models are subject to a number of both qualitative and quantitative conditions. The minimum conditions are set out below.

The CAD document also includes the ability to use internal models to calculate Value at Risk. The BIS minimum qualitative and quantitative standards also apply, but the final capital charge is calculated slightly differently. The minimum standards also apply to other models approved under the CAD, such as risk aggregation models.

10.5.1 Qualitative Standards

The qualitative requirements are to ensure that all the necessary controls are in place to have confidence that the risk management systems are conceptually sound and implemented with integrity. If these controls are not fully met, then the supervisors will not use the minimum multiplication factor. Consequently, the standards are set out in full below.

(a) The institution should have an independent risk control unit that is responsible for the design and implementation of the institution's risk management system. The unit should produce and analyse daily reports on the output of the institution's risk measurement model, including an evaluation of the relationship between measures of risk exposure and trading limits. The unit must be independent from business trading units and should report directly to senior management of the institution.

(b) The unit must conduct a regular back-testing programme, i.e. an ex-post comparison of the risk measure generated by the model against actual daily changes in portfolio value over longer periods of time, as well as hypothetical changes based on static positions.

(c) The board of directors and senior management must be actively involved in the risk control process and must regard risk control as an essential aspect of its business to which sufficient resources need to be devoted. In this regard, the daily reports prepared by the independent risk control unit must be reviewed by a level of management with sufficient seniority and authority to enforce both reductions of positions taken by individual traders and reductions in the institution's overall risk exposure.

(d) The institution's internal risk measurement model must be closely integrated into the day-to-day risk management process of the institution. Its output should accordingly be an integral part of the process of planning, monitoring and controlling the institution's market risk profile.

(e) The risk measurement system should be used in conjunction with internal trading and exposure limits. In this regard, trad-

ing limits should be related to the institution's risk measurement model in a manner that is consistent over time and that
is well understood by both traders and senior management.

(f) A routine and rigorous programme of stress testing should
be in place as a supplement to the risk analysis based on the
day-to-day output of the institution's risk measurement
model. The results of stress testing should be reviewed peri-
odically by senior management and should be reflected in
the policies and limits set by management and the board of
directors. Where stress tests reveal particular vulnerability
to a given set of circumstances, prompt steps should be taken
to manage those risk appropriately (e.g. by hedging against
that outcome or reducing the size of the exposures).

(g) The institution should have a routine in place for ensuring
compliance with a documented set of internal policies, controls and procedures concerning the operation of the risk
measurement system. The institution's risk measurement
system must be well documented, for example through a risk
management manual that describes the basic principles of
the risk management system and provides an explanation of
the empirical techniques used to measure market risk.

(h) An independent review of the risk measurement system
should be carried out regularly in the institution's own internal auditing process. This review should include both the
activities of the business trading units and of the independent risk control unit. A review of the overall risk management process should take place at regular intervals (ideally
not less than once a year) and should specifically address, at
a minimum:

• the adequacy of the documentation of the risk management system and process;
• the organization of the risk control unit;
• the integration of market risk measures into daily risk management;
• the approval process for risk pricing models and valuation systems used by front and back-office personnel;
• the validation of any significant change in the risk measurement process;

- the scope of market risks captured by the risk measurement model;
- the integrity of the management information system;
- the accuracy and completeness of position data;
- the verification of the consistency, timeliness and reliability of data sources used to run models, including the independence of such data sources;
- the accuracy and appropriateness of volatility and correlation assumptions;
- the accuracy of valuation and risk transformation calculations;
- the verification of the model's accuracy through frequent back-testing.

These minimum qualitative standards are also a useful set of criteria to ensure that the risk management system of the institution has been properly established.

10.5.2 Quantitative Standards.

If the institution wishes to use its own internal models to compute Value at Risk and thereby derive a capital requirement, the calculation must also meet a number of quantitative standards. The minimum standards are set out in full below.

(a) Value at Risk must be computed on a daily basis.

(b) In calculating the Value at Risk, 99th percentile, one-tailed confidence interval is to be used.

(c) In calculating Value at Risk, an instantaneous price shock equivalent to a 10-day movement in prices is to be used, i.e.the minimum holding period will be 10 trading days. Institutions may use Value at Risk numbers calculated according to shorter holding periods scaled up to 10 days by the square root of time (for the treatment of options, see point (h) below).

(d) The choice of historical observation period (sample period) for calculating Value at Risk will be constrained to a minimum length of one year. For institutions that use a weighting scheme or other methods for the historical observation period, the `effective' observation period must be at least one year (that is, the weighted average time lag of the individual observations cannot be less than six months).

(e) Institutions should update their data sets no less frequently than once every three months and should also reassess them whenever market prices are subject to material changes. The supervisory body may also require an institution to calculate its Value at Risk using a shorter observation period if, in the supervisor's judgement, this is justified by a significant upsurge in price volatility.

(f) No particular type of model is prescribed. So long as each model captures all the material risks run by the institution, institutions will be free to use models based, for example, on variance/covariance matrices, historical simulations, or Monte Carlo simulations.

(g) Institutions will have discretion to recognize empirical correlations within broad risk categories (e.g. interest rates, exchange rates, equity prices and commodity prices, including related options volatilities in each risk factor category). The supervisory authority may also recognize empirical correlations across broad risk factor categories, provided that the supervisory authority is satisfied that the institution's system for measuring correlations is sound and implemented with integrity.

(h) Models used by institutions must accurately capture the unique risks associated with options within each of the broad risk categories. The following criteria apply to the measurement of options risk:
- models used by banks must capture the non-linear price characteristics of options positions;
- institutions are expected to ultimately move towards the application of a full 10-day price shock to options positions or positions that display option-like characteristics. In the interim, national authorities may require institutions to adjust their capital measure for options risk through other methods, e.g. periodic simulations or stress testing;
- each institution's risk measurement system must have a set of risk factors that captures the volatilities of the rates and prices of the underlying option positions, i.e. Vega risk.

Institutions with relatively large and/or complex options portfolios should have detailed specifications of the relevant volatilities. This means that institutions should measure volatilities of options positions broken down by different maturities.

(i)   Each institution must meet, on a daily basis, a capital requirement expressed as the higher of, firstly its previous day's Value at Risk number measured according to the parameters specified in this section, and secondly an average of the daily Value at Risk measures on each of the preceding sixty business days, multiplied by a multiplication factor.

(j)   The multiplication factor wil be set by individual supervisory authorities on the basis of their assessment of the quality of the institution's risk management system, subject to an absolute minimum of three. Institutions will be required to add to this factor a 'plus' factor directly related to the ex-post performance of the model, thereby introducing a built-in positive incentive to maintain the high predictive quality of the model. The plus factor will range from 0 to 1, based on the outcome of the back-testing that will be required. If the back-testing results are satisfactory and the institution meets all the qualitative standards, the plus factor could be zero.

(k)   Institutions using models will be subject to a separate capital charge to cover the specific risk of interest rate related instruments and equity securities as defined in the standardized approach to the extent that this is not incorporated into their models. However, for institutions using models, the total specific risk charge applied to interest rate related instruments or to equities should in no case be less than half the specific risk charges calculated according to the standardized methodology.

10.5.3 Effects of Using Internal Models

The requirements embodied in BIS Standard (i) above will usually result in a significantly increased measure of risk as compared to the daily Value at Risk calculation. Only in those periods when the institution dramatically increases its market risk exposure is the daily Value at Risk number likely be greater than three times the 60-day rolling average. Thus the capital requirement will usually be three times the 60-day rolling average Value at Risk.

The CAD implementation document adds another complexity to the method of calculating capital when internal models are used. On two randomly chosen dates each year, the institution will have to calculate its capital requirements by both the standard CAD method and by its own Value at Risk method. From these two calculations, a multiplication factor can be derived, which will be changed shortly after the randomly-chosen dates twice each year. The capital requirement will then be based on the higher of the CAD capital requirement based on the institution's calculation of Value at Risk scaled by the multiplication factor and the BIS Value at Risk capital requirement as set out in the BIS method above.

It would appear that the use of internal Value at Risk models will be of little benefit to any institution that has an approved risk aggregation model which reduces the risk on thousands of transactions down to the risk of dozens of transactions. The netting implicit in the correct aggregation of risk will reduce the capital requirements by some two orders of magnitude, and it would appear that attempts to net down the risk any further will be counterbalanced by the multiplication factors required in the use of internal models.

The exception to this statement may be for portfolios in which there is substantial interest rate risk in different currencies. The standard methods, even with the use of equivalent portfolios or risk aggregation models, are run currency by currency, and the resultant capital requirements are then summed to obtain the total capital requirement. This assumes that interest rates are either plus 100% correlated or minus 100% correlated, whichever gives the largest capital requirement. This method is specifically stated in both the BIS proposal and the CAD document. However, in the BIS proposal, where internal models are approved, there is definitely an ability to take correlations into account both within market factor groups and between market factor groups.

When everything is taken into consideration, the biggest problem faced in the implementation of an internal model to calculate the Value at Risk is the question of how to handle options. Value at Risk has to be calculated at the 10-day 99% confidence level. For non-option portfolios, Value at Risk can be calculated at the one-day 99% confidence level, and then scaled up by the square root of 10 to obtain the appropriate Value at Risk. The capital requirement is then this Value at Risk times the scaling factor, which is a factor of at least three.

For option portfolios, the 10-day 99% confidence level is a 2.33 standard deviation change over the 10 days, which translates into a 7.36 standard deviation change over one day. The probability of a 7.36 standard deviation change in a normal distribution is approximately 1 in 10^{13}. As discussed earlier, the best method of calculating the Value at Risk for a non-linear portfolio is by Monte Carlo simulation. In order to obtain sufficient statistics to estimate a 7.36 standard deviation change with any sort of reliability, the number of simulations needed would be of the order of 10^{16}. Using a high-speed computer workstation, one simulation run takes of the order of one second to compute, even using portfolio-level data. Thus it will take billions of years to perform the necessary number of simulations, which is hardly a viable proposition.

There are two possible solutions to this dilemma. The first solution is to run the simulation forwards 10 days without changing the time to maturity of any of the transactions, thereby scaling time by compressing 10 days into one day. The second solution is to scale the volatilities rather than to scale the time. Instead of calculating the 10-day 99% confidence level Value at Risk with a daily volatility of σ, the one-day 99% confidence level Value at Risk is calculated with all volatilities scaled up by the square root of 10, which is 3.16σ. This will then require only 1,000 simulations to produce a reliable estimate of the Value at Risk, while still taking full account of the non-linearity of the option portfolios. Clearly both of these solutions will require an additional computer run to calculate the capital requirement of the institution in addition to the run required to calculate the Value at Risk at the one-day 97.7% confidence level for the standard risk management procedures of the institution. However, as the two computer programs are almost identical, negligible extra programming resources are needed, so this solution is well within the capabilities of the vast majority of financial institutions.

Index